Mission San Fernando Rey Convento

SOLDIERS SCOUNDRELS, POETS & PRIESTS

Dedicated to

Devon Leigh McLaughlin

SOLDIERS
SCOUNDRELS,
POETS &
PRIESTS

David J. McLaughlin

Pentacle Press

Scottsdale, Arizona

The book includes, at the back, a comprehensive timeline of major events in the history of the California Missions from 1769 – 1848.

Library of Congress Control Number: 2003094457
ISBN 10: 0-9763500-4-1
ISBN 13: 780-9763500-4-0
SAN 255-4860
Publishers Cataloguing-in-Publication available upon request

For further information on this publication and related California Mission products, visit our website at www.missionscalifornia.com To contact the publisher write:

Pentacle Press
P.O. Box 9400
Scottsdale, AZ 85252
Printed in the United States of America
www.pentacle-press.com

✸❧ Acknowledgements

All authors of books about the California Missions are indebted to the research done by early scholars. Hubert Howe Bancroft's seven-volume *History of California* (1886-1890) is a seminal work I consulted. The many publications of the Rev. Zephyrin Engelhardt, O.F.M., particularly *The Franciscans in California* (1897) provides essential source materials for the biographies of those who founded and operated the missions. The updated and expanded study of the early missionaries *Franciscan Missionaries in Hispanic California* (1969) by Fr. Maynard Geiger, O.F.M. was particularly useful in ferreting out facts about some of the less prominent Franciscans.

I was inspired to write this book by some of the early popular accounts of the missions, many now sadly out of print. In particular, the enthusiastic and comprehensive account *California Missions and Historic Landmarks* (1915) by Mrs. A.S.C. Forbes and *California's Spanish Missions* by Spencer Crump (1975).

I am indebted to Michael R. Hardwick for the idea of focusing on key historic figures. His short monographs on prominent Spanish officials are well researched and concisely written. Michael was also quite generous in recommending primary source material on Alta California governors.

The 1979 Sunset Pictorial *The California Missions*, profusely illustrated, tells the story of the missions very effectively. This book helped me in selecting the historic figures to feature in the 30 biographies. I also came to trust *The Spell of California's Spanish Colonial Missions* (2001) by Donald

Francis Toomey. His research on the history of each mission is impeccable and the best source I found on Hispanic devotional art.

I was able to assemble early photographs of the missions with the help of Pat Hathaway, (www.caviews.com) whose extensive collection of vintage photographs of California is without parallel. Many early drawings and historic photographs of the missions can be viewed online. Particularly useful were the digital archives at the Bancroft Library at University of California at Berkeley, the California Museum of Photography at UC Riverside and the Library of Congress. I particularly took inspiration from George Fiskes' early photographs of Mission Carmel, surrounded by open land, with a clear view of the sea. The individuals who painted the missions at the turn of the 20th century were another source of inspiration, particularly the large oil paintings of the missions by Edwin Deakin, some of which are on display at the Los Angeles County Museum of Natural History.

California Mission Studies Association (CMSA) is a non-profit group dedicated to the study and preservation of the missions. Their annotated links to websites related to the missions are an invaluable resource. I am proud to be a sustaining member of the association.

An outstanding group of professionals helped me design, format and publish *Soldiers, Scoundrels, Poets & Priests* in the original digital version. I am indebted to Laureen Mauer (graphic design), David Reuter (copy editing) and Barry Doyle (all manner of technical advice and help). I want to also thank Ellen Reid, Dotti Albertine, Laren Bright and Sharon Tully for their invaluable assistance in helping design, lay out and produce this high quality print version of the book.

Finally I want to thank my family for supporting me in this 18-month effort, particularly my daughter Devon, who accompanied me on several trips to the missions and my wife, Bradley, who was always my last resort when I needed objective feedback.

❧ About the Author

DAVID J. MCLAUGHLIN is a writer, photographer and business consultant. He has a Master of Arts degree from Fordham University. He lives in Phoenix, Arizona. McLaughlin is the author of *The Executive Money Map* (McGraw Hill, 1976), *Storefronts: A Travel Journal* (in the Long Road Home, 2001), *Images of the California Missions* (Pentacle Press, 2003), and three full color guide books which he co-authored with Laren Bright: *Around the Quabbin* (2005), *Exploring the Upper Pioneer Valley* (2006), and *Along the Mohawk Trail* (2006). McLaughlin is a member of the California Mission Studies Association.

Steve Thompson

Mission Carmel by George Fiske.

🦋 Introduction

Read no history: Nothing but biography, for that is life without theory.
—BENJAMIN DISRAELI

The real story of the California Missions is told in the lives of people—the missionaries and Spanish soldiers who settled the wilderness of Alta California; the Native Americans who did all the work and the Indian leaders who resisted destruction of their way of life. Also, the sea captains who traded manufactured goods for mission-produced hides and tallow; the Mexican officials who plundered the mission lands and property before American takeover of California; the novelists, poets, artists and early photographers at the turn of the 20th century who created a nostalgia for a romanticized Spanish past and a keen public interest in preserving these historic structures.

We know the names of a few of the famous personalities featured in this book—Junipero Serra, the missionary founder; Richard Henry Dana, who wrote of the "hide trade" in *Two Years Before The Mast*; John Charles Fremont, the pathfinder whose behind the scene maneuvering helped win California for the United States; and William Randolph Hearst who had a hunting lodge a couple miles from Mission San Antonio de Padua.

But who today remembers Franciso Hermenegildo Garces, also known as the " . . . Daniel Boone in Franciscan garb," who died at his post in 1781, knowing an attack on his mission was all but certain; or Felipe Arroyo de la Cuesta, who fulfilled his contract of 10 years of missionary service, so crippled he could hardly walk, but stayed another 20 years because there was no one to replace him? Who remembers Estanislao, a neophyte from the San Jose Mission who led a large-scale revolt of hundreds of mission Indians in 1828, or the rascal, Pio Pico, the last Mexican-era governor who was still selling off mission buildings in 1846 a few days before Commodore John Sloat sailed into Monterey Bay with the Pacific Fleet?

What stories these old walls tell. Colonial Spain's greatest love story took place within the walls of the San Francisco Presidio in 1806, when a Russian count, seeking supplies to save that nation's colony in Alaska, fell in love with a comely Spanish maiden . . . and died tragically in the wilds of Siberia on his way to seek permission to marry. The only pirate attack on the West Coast of the United States occurred in 1818 when two ships under the command of Hipolite Bouchard attacked and burned Monterey and Mission San Juan Capistrano. California's first mass murder occurred in 1848 at Mission San Miguel, when a band of five ruffians killed 12 members of the William Reed family.

The 30 biographies in this book can be read on many levels. Collectively, they tell the real story of missions. Individually they inspire, educate, and entertain. The men and women who figure prominently in the 230-year history of the old Spanish missions led lives worth knowing. Their stories are organized into three parts: The founding and development of the missions by Spain (1779-1821,) the era when California was a territory of Mexico (1821-1848) and the century and a half of American rule, which saw the decline and ultimate rebirth of the historic structures.

❧ Table of Contents

1   **The Spanish**

7   CHAPTER 1 **Juan Rodriguez Cabrillo**—Conquistador who explored and mapped the coast of California in 1542.

15   CHAPTER 2 **Gaspar de Portola**—Leader of the expedition that settled Alta California in 1769.

23   CHAPTER 3 **Junipero Serra**—Franciscan priest who founded the first nine missions and served as Father President from 1769 to his death in 1784.

31   CHAPTER 4 **Juan Bautista de Anza**—Spanish pathfinder who established the first overland trail to California in 1774-1775.

39   CHAPTER 5 **Philipe de Neve**—The first Governor of the Californias, who created the system under which California was governed.

47   CHAPTER 6 **Pedro Yanunali**—Chief of the Chumash, who supported the Spanish presence in Santa Barbara and ultimately converted to Christianity.

55   CHAPTER 7 **Francisco Hermenegildo Garces**—Franciscan pathfinder and martyr.

61   CHAPTER 8 **Manual Ruiz and Estevan Munras**—The architect who designed and built the Mission Carmel church and the Royal Presidio chapel in Monterey, and the Spanish artist who created the stunning interior of the Mission San Miguel church.

69 CHAPTER 9 **Nikolai Petrovich Rezanov**—The Russian Count who sailed to San Francisco in 1806 seeking supplies, fell in love with the daughter of the Commandant and died a tragic death in Siberia on his way home to seek permission to marry.

75 CHAPTER 10 **Hipolite Bouchard**—The French privateer sailing under the flag of Argentina who attacked the coast of California in 1818, burning the Monterey Presidio and Mission San Juan Capistrano.

83 **The Mexicans**

89 CHAPTER 11 **Filipe Arroyo de la Cuesta**—The inspiring and talented Franciscan missionary who spent 25 years building Mission San Juan Bautista, and who stayed at his post after Mexican takeover even though crippled with rheumatism.

95 CHAPTER 12 **Estanislao**—An exceptional Indian neophyte from Mission San Jose, who led the largest and most successful revolt against the mission system in 1828.

101 CHAPTER 13 **Mariano Guadalupe Vallejo**—The soldier statesman who controlled Sonoma and northern California during Mexican rule and facilitated the takeover of California by the Americans in 1846-48.

111 CHAPTER 14 **William Edward Petty Hartnell**—One of the early hide and tallow traders, who became a Mexican citizen, protected the missions and founded the first school of higher education in California.

119 CHAPTER 15 **Auguste Duhaut-Cilly**—A French sea captain who visited California in 1827-28, and documented his observations in a published journal.

125 CHAPTER 16 **Jedediah Strong Smith**—The legendary

mountain man, who was the first American to visit Alta California by land in 1826-27.

133 CHAPTER 17 **Richard Henry Dana**—The author of *Two Years Before the Mast*, who visited Alta California as a young sailor in 1834-35.

141 CHAPTER 18 **Narciso Duran**—The last great leader of the mission chain, who kept the mission network functioning after their secularization by Mexico in 1833-34.

149 CHAPTER 19 **Don Antonio Aguirre**—A successful importer who supported the missions and the Catholic Church in its darkest days.

155 CHAPTER 20 **Pio Pico**—The last, and most corrupt governor of California during the Mexican era, who was still selling mission property days before the Americans occupied Monterey in July 1846.

161 **The Americans**

167 CHAPTER 21 **John Charles Fremont**—The American army officer and pathfinder who charted trails to the west and played a decisive role in the American takeover of California.

175 CHAPTER 22 **Charles Fletcher Lummis**—Newspaperman and promoter of California who founded the Land-marks Club in 1895, dedicated to restoring the missions and other historic California structures.

183 CHAPTER 23 **Helen Hunt Jackson**—Indian rights activist and author whose best selling romantic novel. *Ramona* laid the groundwork for broad public support for the preservation of the old Spanish missions.

195   CHAPTER 24 **Mission Painters**—Henry Chapman Ford, Christian August Jorgensen and Edwin Deakin, three painters of exceptional talent who produced stunning images of the old missions.

201   CHAPTER 25 **Mission Photographers**—Pioneering masters of the new medium of photography whose images of the old missions captivated the general public between1885-1920.

207   CHAPTER 26 **Mrs. A.S.C. Forbes**—Writer and civic leader who led the effort to preserve El Camino Real and mark the historic trail with guidepost bells.

213   CHAPTER 27 **John Steven McGroarty**—The author of the long-running, *The Mission Play*, a three-hour extravaganza that told the story of the founding, success and ultimate decline of the missions.

221   CHAPTER 28 **William Randolph Hearst**—Newspaper magnate. Hearst was a generous contributor to the missions throughout his long, controversial life.

229   CHAPTER 29 **Joseph Jacinto "Jo" Mora**—Sculptor who created the sarcophagus of Junipero Serra at Mission Carmel.

235   CHAPTER 30 **Harry Downie**—The gifted artisan and master mission restorer who dedicated 50 years of his life to the restoration of Mission Carmel and led the drive for the authentic restoration of these unique treasures.

234   *Image Sources and Credits*
241   *California Mission Glossary*
253   *California Mission Timeline*
258   *References*
259   *Index*

THE SPANISH

1769-1821

Spanish Franciscans established 21 missions along the coast of Alta California beginning in 1769. After years of struggle and Indian resistance, substantial numbers were converted and the missions become economically self-sufficient, controlling the best agricultural and pasture land in California. As the Spanish colonies in the Americas revolted, and Spain became embroiled in wars in Europe, support for the missions declined and Alta California ultimately became a territory of Mexico in 1821.

Intrepid pathfinders, Spanish authorities and a band of courageous missionaries emerge as the central figures in the first 52 years of Alta California. Our story begins with a conquistador, **Juan Rodriguez Cabrillo**, the man who discovered the Bay of San Diego and first charted the California coast for Spain in 1542.

Disappointed by the apparent lack of gold in the lands north and west of New Spain (Mexico), the Spaniards left the wilderness of Alta California alone for the next 230 years.

Other foreign powers coveted California however. The English explorer Francis Drake had actually made port in San Francisco in 1579, after successfully raiding Spanish treasure galleons. He claimed the land for England, but nothing came of it.

As the years passed, the biggest threat to Spanish dominance became the push of fur trappers from Russia into California from bases in Alaska and present day Oregon. When Russian trappers began to appear north of San Francisco, the Spanish decided that they had to colonize and fortify this territory, or risk losing it. In 1769, after years of careful planning, the Spanish finally acted. Spanish expeditions left Mexico in early 1769 with the objective of establishing three missions. The land and sea parties met near the spot Cabrillo discovered two centuries earlier, and built temporary structures on a hill overlooking San Diego Bay. The man in charge of the expedition was a Catalonian soldier of noble rank, **Don Gaspar de Portola**. He succeeded against all odds. Only about 100 of the original expedition of 219 survived, but they established a toehold in California.

Over the next year Portola explored the coast, established presidios in San Diego and Monterey and organized the new colony. An experienced missionary priest, **Junipero Serra,** founded the San Diego mission in 1769 and then sailed up the coast in 1770 to found Mission San Carlos Borromeo de Carmelo.

As soon as Serra could assemble the necessary supplies and men, the missions begin to spread out from the ports of San Diego and Monterey, with San Antonio de Padua and San Gabriel being established in 1771.

These early missions were less than perfect in terms of locations. The initial locations often proved impractical, with both of the first two missions being moved later. The initial San Diego site had little water, and there were few Indians nearby. Therefore, it was moved six miles inland. Mission Carmel was located too close to the presidio, and it also had to be relocated.

By end of their first decade in California, the Spanish had established eight missions, but supplying them by sea proved difficult. **Juan Bautista de Anza** was commissioned to discover a land route to Alta California. De Anza was an accomplished soldier who won fame fighting the Apaches in the Sonoma territory. He laid out the trail in 1774, and led a group of 300 settlers to the new territory in 1775. The soldiers who accompanied de Anza on these adventures became the founders and first settlers of San Francisco.

A lack of coordination between the military and Franciscans during the early years complicated matters. Alta California was under the authority of a military governor in Loreto, in Baja California. Serra returned to Mexico City to clarify his authority and get more support for the missions. In 1777, in recognition of then growing importance of Alta California, the seat of government was shifted to Monterey. The first governor of Alta and Baja California was **Philipe de Neve,** a dynamic leader who founded the pueblos (towns) of San Jose and Los Angeles, built the presidio at Santa Barbara and reorganized the finances and administration of the territory.

The coastal area from present day Malibu to the southern edge of Monterey County was the land of the Chumash, a talented, intelligent tribe who proved receptive to Christianity. Nave's decision to settle this area in 1782 with a mission (San Buenaventura) and presidio (Santa Barbara) solidified the Spanish position. The support of **Pedro Yanunali**, who ruled 13 Chumash Indian villages in the Santa Barbara area proved critical. The Chumash supported the Europeans in the early years, but the fate of the tribe over the years of Spanish occupation is heart rendering.

Over the first decades of Spanish settlement the missions evolved from a cluster of dirt huts to fully developed complex of buildings, typically organized in a quadrangle. The missions were self-contained villages of a 1,000 or more residents, including two Franciscan padres, four to five soldiers and the Indian converts, called neophytes.

The driving force behind all of the successful missions was a Franciscan who needed to be an inspiring leader, a model priest and the skilled administrator of a complex community.

Not all the Franciscans lived to see the ultimate success of the mission system. There was a high death rate among the missionaries – isolated in remote areas with no medical facilities. Many of the first missions were repeatedly attacked. One of the priests who lost his life during these early years was **Francisco Hermenegildo Garces**, killed in 1781 during an Indian uprising. Garces, called a "Daniel Boone in Franciscan garb" by a noted historian, played a key role in the charting and settlement of California before his death.

Gradually over the years the missions grew from struggling institutions, whose survival was often in doubt, to successful enterprises. By 1799, the 30-year anniversary of the Spanish in Alta California, 18 missions had been established and a 19th (Santa Ines) was planned.

As the economic prosperity of the mission chain increased, architects and skilled workmen were brought in from Mexico to help design and build the churches into the magnificent structures known today. **Manuel Ruiz**, an architect and master mason, arrived in Monterey in 1791. Ruiz designed and built the Royal Chapel at the Monterey Presidio, and the architecturally acclaimed church at the Carmel Mission, which was dedicated in 1797. Another exceptional Spanish artist, **Estevan Munras,** decorated the interior of San Miguel in 1820.

California was beginning to attract notable foreign visitors by the 1790s. The drawings and diaries of the early visitors present early sketches of mission life. While most of the early travellers were French or British sea captains, in 1806 **Count Nikolai Petrovich Rezanov** sailed into the harbor of San Francisco, seeking food and supplies for the starving Russian colony at Sitka, Alaska. During his stay he became betrothed to the young daughter of the presidio commandant. The unrequited love of Nikolai and Conchita (he died in

Siberia on his way home to secure permission to marry) has endured in story and song.

Unfortunately developments that would portend the end of the mission system began to manifest themselves at the beginning of the 19th century. Spain was engaged in European wars that diverted resources and attention from California. To make matters worst, Spain's colonies in the Americas were revolting against Spanish rule. The rebellion in Mexico began in 1810.

The missions got caught up in the geo-political struggles of the times. As supply ships became infrequent, the missions were forced to trade their hides and tallow for finished goods, and in the process, opened up the territory to French, British and American interests. The Monterey Presidio and Mission San Juan Capistrano were burned in 1818 by the privateer **Hipolite Bouchard,** who flew the flag of Argentina, then struggling to free itself from Spanish control.

After years of uncertainty and rumor, the Spanish lost control of New Spain in 1821. The missions entered into a new and troubling period.

Monterey Presidio—Juan Rodriguez Cabrillo explored the coast of California in 1542, reaching as far north as San Francisco. When the Spanish settled Alta California in 1769-70, they established forts in Monterey and San Diego.

CHAPTER 1

JUAN RODRIGUEZ CABRILLO

Conquistador who explored and mapped
the coast of California in 1542

Three Spanish ships under the command of Juan Rodriguez Cabrillo, on Sept. 28, 1542, entered the waters of an area now known as San Diego Bay. He anchored his flagship, the San Salvador, on a small finger of land near the mouth of the bay. The Spaniards wondered about the "great smokes" they saw from their ships. They learned that the natives of the area, the Kumeyaay, burned part of the land each fall to enrich the soil and help next year's crop.

Cabrillo's party had some contact with the natives, mostly distributing trinkets. The contacts weren't always friendly. These San Diego area Indians would prove to be out-right hostile when a mission was established on a large hill overlooking the bay, two centuries later.

After a few days rest, Cabrillo sailed up the coast of Alta California. Periodically he would stop and claim possession of the land for the King of Spain. The Indians who observed the ceremony must have been puzzled when the strange group of white men would cut down a tree, move rocks around it and pour water over the marker.

Over the next two months Cabrillo explored the bay of San Pedro, which would turn out to be a prominent storage area for hides and a transportation depot during the Mission era. On Oct. 10 they arrived at an Indian town with "large houses," now present-day Santa Barbara. The explorers found the Chumash Indians confident and curious. As the Indians grew more comfortable with the Spaniards, they would paddle their canoes, called tomols, out to the ships and trade. The Chumash would later prove to be very receptive to Christianity.

The expedition continued up the coast to a spot near present day San Simeon, where a violent storm on Nov. 11, damaged the smaller ships. The San Salvador continued to sail north and reached San Francisco, but missed the large bay opening. The crew turned back to rejoin the rest of the fleet near present day Santa Cruz.

Cabrillo wintered in the Channel Islands, off Santa Barbara. Unfortunately the natives had grown uneasy about the continued presence of the Spaniards, and began small-scale attacks. During one of the skirmishes Cabrillo was injured leading a rescue party. The wound became gangrenous, and Cabrillo died Jan. 2, 1543.

Command of the expedition passed to Chief Pilot Bartolome Ferrer who attempted to continue the exploration up the coast, with little success. The three storm-battered ships made their way back down the coast and headed home.

So who was this daring explorer Juan Cabrillo?

Not too much is known of Cabrillo's early years. He was born in Europe, probably Portugal, in the 1490s, around the time the Spanish were finally successful in driving the Moors out of their country. Many of the Spanish noblemen who led that successful fight immigrated to the Americas in search of new adventures. Cabrillo was one of the thousands of Iberians who flocked to the New World seeking, as one conquistador put it "to serve God and also get rich."

Some historians believe that Cabrillo's initial service in the New World may have been in the bloody conquest of Cuba. They also believe that Cabrillo learned to become a boat builder while in Cuba. Other historians assert that he was a teen-ager and apprentice boat builder in Cuba, not a soldier. In any event, Cabrillo first emerges in written records as a Captain of Crossbows in the army of Hernan Cortez, the conquistador who invaded the Aztec empire (present day Mexico.) Cabrillo fought in several battles during the campaign. He played a major role in the construction and sealing of 13 small ships, called bergantines, which Cortez used in the siege of Tenochtitlan in 1521. He was wounded during the Tenochtitlan battle.

Juan Cabrillo

After Mexico fell, Cabrillo was sent on various expeditions. He became a senior captain in the army of Pedro de Alvarado. He fought for 12 years in the conquest of Honduras, Guatemala and El Salvador. Sometime early in the campaign in Guatemala, Cabrillo took an Indian "wife" and fathered three daughters, each of whom would marry a conquistador. In 1527 he was one of the founders of Santiago, Guatemala, and soon became one of its leading and wealthiest citizens.

In 1532, Cabrillo, who was then in his late 30s, decided that he was ready to take an "official" wife. He traveled to Spain where he courted and married Beatriz Sanchez de Ortega, the younger sister of a friend. He and Beatrice returned to Santiago in the summer of 1533. The King had made his mentor, Alvarado, governor of Guatemala. Cabrillo assisted Alvarado in quelling a rebellion in Honduras in 1536, for which he was granted "the pueblos of Teota and Cotela, with all its senores, Indians, barrios and fields." He was also appointed Chief Magistrate of the seaport of Aztapa and

9

VICEROY MENDOZA . . . recalled from Guatemala a much experienced fighter, entrepreneur and ship-owner . . . one Juan Rodriguez Cabrillo, and instructed him to navigate north beyond California.

. . . This would be a terrible voyage, running against currents, winds and heavy seas, close by fog-blanketed, perilously rocky shores.

Cabrillo's square-rigged flagship, the San Salvador, which he owned and probably had built, was a slim galleon of high sterncastle and lower forecastle measuring about a 100 feet, with a carrying capacity of 200 tons. Incredibly, she crawled with nearly a 100 people: Four officers, 20 to 30 sailors, about as many black and Indian slaves, two or three cabin boys, 25 soldiers, Augustinian Fray Julian de Lescano, and a few merchants. ❧ From *Spain in the Southwest* by John L. Kessel

ordered to oversee construction of a fleet for exploration of the Pacific.

Over several years Cabrillo built a fleet, at least six or seven ships under his personal direction. By the summer of 1540 the fleet was ready to sail after a final fitting in El Salvador. Alvarado's instructions from Spain were to explore the vast largely unexplored land north of the Spanish colonies. Rumors abounded of fabulously wealthy cities—the Seven Cities of Cibola.

Another revolt in Honduras, an earthquake that destroyed Santiago and the untimely death of Alvarado, delayed the start of the expedition.

In 1542, the Viceroy asked Cabrillo to reassemble the ships and prepare for two expeditions. One group was to explore the Pacific, the other, under Cabrillo's command, was to sail up the California coast. The ships were prepared for a two-year journey.

The goal of the Cabrillo expedition was to discover hordes of gold and also open up a path to the Orient. The people of this time had that no idea of the vastness of the Pacific Ocean, and thought the land above the Spanish colonies curved directly into China.

Cabrillo's ships sailed out of Navidad harbor on June 27, 1542. They were fated to return a scant seven months later, with Cabrillo dead.

After news of Cabrillo's death reached Guatemala, greedy rivals seized much of his property. His widow and son spent most of the rest of their lives trying to recoup his wealth. The case wasn't settled until 1617, and little was returned to his heirs.

Cabrillo's expedition was considered a failure at the time, since he didn't find gold or a route to the Orient. His charts and journal didn't arrive in Madrid for 16 years, so the authorities didn't realize the full significance of his discoveries.

The results of Cabrillo's journey, though, had a profound impact on Spanish policy. The Cabrillo expedition confirmed that no more gold-rich civilizations were likely to be found in the land north and west of Mexico. It also became clear that the territory the Spanish called Alta California was a wilderness, almost impossible to reach by ship, and thus difficult to colonize. New Spain would leave the area alone for 230 years.

When the Spanish finally began to settle Alta California, the maps and records of the Cabrillo expedition became critical. The first mission would be sited in San Diego, near the bay that Cabrillo discovered in 1842. Recalling the difficulty Cabrillo had sailing up the coast, the expedition that founded California hedged their bets by sending a land expedition as well as two ships. Many of the locations Cabrillo noted in his journey became the site of future missions—San Diego, San Buenaventura, Santa Barbara, Santa Cruz and San Francisco.

Model of a Ventureno (Chumash) Indian Village along the California Coast
Source: Author's photograph of a display in Ventura County Museum

About sixty Indian tribes lived in what is the present state of California at the time of the arrival of the Europeans. The Chumash were the first major group of California Indians to be discovered. Cabrillo landed near the present site of the city of Ventura on October 10, 1542.

REFERENCES:

Cabrillo by Nancy Lemke, San Luis Obispo: EZ Nature Books, 1991 An interesting, well written summary of the life of the explorer. The author illustrates this paperback with maps and more than 50 small sketches.

The Conquistadors by Michael Wood, University of California Press, 2001. Fascinating stories of men who conquered the New World for Spain.

Encyclopedia of Discovery and Exploration. Multi-volume reference series. London: Aldus Books, 1977 Comprehensive.

The Cabrillo Era and His Voyage of Discovery by Carl F. Reupsch. San Diego: Cabrillo Historical Association, 1982. This excellent summary of Cabrillo's exploits was published by the non-profit group that supports the Cabrillo National Monument.

Juan Rodriguez Cabrillo by Harry Kelsey, Huntington Library: San Marino, CA, 1986. An impressive scholarly work.

13

First Mass—Monterey

This painting depicts the celebratory mass held on the shores of Monterey Bay on June 3, 1770, when the Monterey Presidio and Church (originally built next to the presidio) were founded.

CHAPTER 2

GASPAR de PORTOLA

Leader of the expedition that settled
Alta California in 1769

When Russian trappers built an outpost on the Farallon Island off San Francisco, it became clear that the remote wilderness of Alta California would have to be settled or lost to Czarist Russia.

Spain had very little knowledge of the land that was to become the last outpost of the Spanish empire. Only the seacoast had been mapped and that incompletely. The known facts were discouraging: Sailing up the coast against strong prevailing headwinds was difficult and dangerous; there was no known land route from existing Spanish settlements; the native inhabitants were numerous and many were hostile.

The Spanish authorities dusted off old plans, retrieved all known maps from the archives and started to organize an expedition. Inspector General Jose de Galvez, the King's personal representative in New Spain, did the detailed planning. Galvez decided that there would be twin land and sea parties: Two ships, followed later by a supply ship, would depart at different times from La Paz and rendezvous with two land expeditions at the bay of San Diego, the harbor discovered by Cabrillo in 1542. The bay was about halfway between Loreto, the seat of government for the Californias, and Monterey, targeted to become the headquarters of Alta California. The expeditionary force would build a presidio and a mission at

San Diego, then proceed up the coast to the bay of Monterey. There they would establish the second presidio and mission.

Volunteering to lead the expedition was Don Gaspar de Portola. Portola had impeccable credentials for the job. He had served successfully as a soldier for Spain in Italy and Portugal. He had just completed the delicate and controversial task of expelling the Jesuits from the missions of Baja California, replacing them with Franciscans. Most importantly, he was a member of the Spanish nobility, born in Catalonia in 1734. While the designation "Don" was applied more informally in New Spain and later in Alta California to any man of means and influence, its use in Spain was strictly restricted to nobility.

THE FIRST DAY

Diary of the journey made by land to the ports of San Diego and Monterey . . .

The expedition was composed of 37 soldiers in leather jackets with their captain, Don Fernando de Rivera. This officer was sent in advance with 27 soldiers and I followed with 10 men and a sergeant.

The 11th day of May, (1769,) I set out from Santa Maria, the last mission to the north, escorted by four soldiers, in company with Father Junipero Serra, president of the missions, and Father Miguel Campa. This day we proceeded for about four hours with very little water for the animals and without any pasture, which obliged us to go on farther in the afternoon to find some. There was, however, no water.

On the 12th we proceeded over a good road for five hours and halted at a place called La Poza de Agua Dulce. Again, no pasture.

🦋 From the Journal of Gaspar de Portola

The Portola expedition set out in January 1769. The ships arrived in San Diego in April, but they were in dreadful shape. The San Carlos, which had left La Paz first, was at sea for 110 days. It had encountered heavy headwinds, overshot the San

Diego harbor because of an error on the charts, and had to make its way back south. The San Antonio was at sea for 54 days, and arrived before the San Carlos. The supply ship, carrying the bulk of the provisions, never arrived.

Over a third of the crew had died, mostly from scurvy, a disease that rotted gums and affected joints and muscles. The British had discovered that scurvy was prevented and cured by adding fresh fruit and a vegetable to a sailor's diet, but this remedy was not yet widely known.

The two land expeditions departed after the ships had left. The first party headed by Capt. Fernando Rivera y Moncada, and accompanied by Father Juan Crespi (who was also diarist for the expedition,) left in April with a large pack train of 180 mules and some 500 domestic animals. Christian Indians accompanied the party, but most of them deserted en route. Crespi described the land as "sterile, arid, lacking grass and water and abounding in stones and thorns."

The second land contingent left in mid-May and was under the direct supervision of Portola. The Portola party had to scrounge for food as it made its way up the Baja peninsula. As Portola recounts in his personal diary, "I was obliged to seize everything I saw as I passed through those poor missions, leaving them, to my keen regret, scantily provided for." Despite the foraging, the party soon ran out of food. The Franciscan who accompanied Portola was Father Junipero Serra, who was destined to go down in history as the founder of California missions. The expeditionary force also included a military engineer and cartographer, Miguel Costanso and surgeon Dr. Pedro Prat.

The land expedition finally arrived on July 1, 1769. Serra was thrilled. He wrote his close friend Father Francisco Palou "I arrived here at the Port of San Diego. It is beautiful to behold, and does not belie its reputation. Here I met all who had set out before me whether by sea or by land—but not the dead."

17

There were a lot of dead—over half of the expeditionary force of 219 had deserted or died. Many of the rest were still sick and little progress had made in establishing a foothold in the hostile territory.

The terrible situation would have discouraged anyone. However, a resolute Portola—with strong encouragement from Serra—decided to press on and fulfill his orders to establish the presidios and establish a colony at Monterey Bay.

Portola ordered the San Antonio to return to San Blas to bring back desperately needed supplies. The ship sailed with a skeleton crew of eight men all that remained of the original complement. Only two of these men were alive when the ship reached San Blas.

The building of San Diego was left to Serra and a small contingent of soldiers. Portola, with a party described as "skeletons who had been spared by scurvy, hunger and thirst," set off overland to make their way through the uncharted wilderness to Monterey, some 350 miles to the north. The group included Portola, Capt. Rivera, Lt. Fages, Crespi, the engineer Costanso, six Catalonian volunteers and 26 soldiers.

They encountered a country of "rocks, brushwood and rugged mountains covered with snow." It took 38 days for Portola to reach Monterey Bay. However, tragically, he did not recognize the bay, which Juan Sebastian Vizcaino erroneously described in 1602 as a large sheltered port, secure against all winds. Scouts were sent out and explored as far north as Santa Cruz. Portola made decision to return to San Diego, declaring his mission incomplete.

He erected a large cross at the unknown bay, and another on the nearby cliffs of Carmel. The cross at Monterey bore the inscription "The overland expedition from San Diego returned from this place . . . starving." To make matters worst, the weather turned bad, and there was little food available. Several times during the return journey one of the mules had to be killed to provide food.

Serra was keenly disappointed when Portola returned, and is reported to have said, "You came from Rome and you did not see the Pope."

Conditions in San Diego itself were desperate. The supply ship San Jose was long overdue and feared lost at sea. Portola ordered Capt. Rivera to return to Baja and bring back supplies. The dwindling remnants of the expedition waited another seven months for relief.

Gaspar de Portola

Portola finally ordered the settlement abandoned, and started to prepare for a return to Baja. The missionaries objected and vowed to stay on their own. Then, miraculously, on the eve of the day of departure the San Antonio sailed into San Diego Bay.

By now convinced by his captains that he had found the Bay of Monterey on his first trip north, Portola returned there overland. Serra followed a few days later on board the San Antonio, arriving in Monterey a week after Portola. On June 3, 1770, Serra consecrated the site of the new mission, dedicated to St. Charles of Borromeo. The soldiers fired their muskets, and cannons on the San Antonio let loose a volley. Serra delivered a sermon and Portola ceremonially claimed the land for Spain.

A temporary presidio and mission built of earth and poles were completed within a month. A small garrison of soldiers under the command of Lt. Don Pedro Fages was left in charge of the presidio. Portola, his task complete, set sail for Mexico on the San Antonio. When he arrived in Mexico City there was a great celebration. Portola became governor of Puebla, Mexico in 1776. He died in Spain in 1784.

Ships departing for Alta California from La Paz—painting done by Walter Francis in 1909. Source: The original is at the Bancroft Library. Black and white copy in author's possession.

In the difficult early years the missions were supplied by ship. The ships were too small (under 200 tons) to carry more than a few months of supplies. The ships were often blown off course and delayed for weeks. Only two ships from the Portola expedition made it to California. All but two of the crew of one ship died.

REFERENCES:

Gaspar de Portola: Explorer and Founder of California by F. Boneau Companies, and translated by Alan K. Brown, Lerida, Spain: Institue de Estudios Herdenses, 1983. The 404-page book on Portola contains much original source material and illustrations.

The California Missions, edited by Dorothy Krell and Paul C. Johnson. Sunset Books Inc.: Menlo Park, CA, 1964 updated 1979. This well-written book contains several chapters that detail the founding of California, and describe the Portola expedition.

Gaspar de Portola, an online biography provided by the San Diego Historical Society. An excellent summary of the expedition http://www.sandiego-history.org/bio/portola/portola.htm

The Portola Expedition of 1769 by Gary S. Breschini, Ph.D. a publication of the Monterey County Historical Society, 2000. An online summary is available at http://users.dedot.com/mchs/portola1769.html

Junipero Serra was ordained a priest, received the degree of Doctor of Philosophy and taught in Palma on the island of Majorca. During his years in Palma Fr. Serra lived at the Franciscan Convento de San Francisco.

CHAPTER 3

JUNIPERO SERRA

Franciscan priest who founded the first nine
missions and served as Father President from
1769 to his death in 1784

One of the last members of the 1769 Gaspar de Portola expedition to reach San Diego was a diminutive Franciscan, who arrived on July 1, slowly making his way along the bay to the Spanish campsite. Sitting awkwardly on a mule, the little priest, only 5-feet 2-inches tall, looked every bit his 57 years. Junipero Serra had traveled up the Baja peninsula by mule, unable to walk more than a few steps because of a swollen foot and leg.

Serra found a badly demoralized band of half-starved men camped out near the shore. He learned that less than half of the 219 who had come by land had made it to California. The supply ship had still not arrived. Most of the crew and half the soldiers on the other two ships had died of scurvy. Serra and Portola organized the survivors, sending out a party to find a source of water and a more protected location to establish the presidio and church. They found a promising site on what is now called Presidio Hill, overlooking San Diego Bay. The soldiers built simple huts and a small church.

There, on July 16, 1769, Serra founded the first California mission, San Diego de Alcala. Capt. Portola and 75 men then marched north to find Monterey Bay. Serra was left in charge of the sick and dying, with a small band of soldiers for protection.

The early days were trying. The Indians attacked the campsite in August, killing Serra's 'servant (a neophyte from Baja) and injuring three others. By fall, the temperature turned colder at night and the Spaniards didn't have the right clothing. Over the next months, several of the remaining survivors died. The group was frequently near starvation. On Jan. 19, 1770 the expedition that had marched north six months earlier returned without having found Monterey Bay. Things couldn't have been worst. Portola considered aborting the mission and returning to New Spain.

After Serra pleaded for more time, Portola decided they would wait six more weeks until the feast of St. Joseph (March 19), then if supplies hadn't arrived, the survivors would march south, back to Baja. On the 19th as the soldiers were packing, a lookout spotted the San Antonio, rounding the tip of Point Loma. The expedition was saved.

Portola left almost immediately for a second, and ultimately successful, attempt to find Monterey. Serra joined him there (sailing up the coast on the San Antonio.) He founded the second mission, San Carlos Borromeo de Carmelo on June 3, 1770 and decided to make Carmel his headquarters.

Over the next decade and a half Serra was the driving force behind the settlement of California. During his lifetime he established seven additional missions and laid plans for 12 more. He traveled the coast almost continuous, logging some 24,000 miles by one calculation. In 1778, he received the faculty to administer the Sacrament of Confirmation (usually reserved for a Bishop), and over the rest of his life, he confirmed 5,309 persons, most of them neophytes.

The ultimate success of Alta California was a team effort, of course. It required the unwavering support of the king, financial backing from New Spain, support from the Missionary College of San Fernando, supply ships willing to make the difficult passage up the coast, a few score of soldiers defending 650 miles of coastline and missionaries willing to live in primitive, isolated outposts in the wilderness. However, like all new ventures, it required a leader with vision, a passionate commitment to success and the personal characteristics needed to inspire others.

Serra was energetic, forceful leader. By all accounts he was a habitually serious man, quiet and austere, not given to frivolous conversation. He was "all religious."

> "I HAD A NOTION, a piece of excusable, self-complacency, that I would be the first among the four who were close to . . . that milestone (1,000 baptisms), but hail to San Diego! . . . I am consoling myself with the thought that by the (end of) April we will reach the mark that San Diego reached in March. But, in either case, may the glory and honor be God's alone."
>
> ❧ In a congratulatory letter to Fermin de Lasuen, April 17, 1784

Serra ate lightly, avoiding meat and wine. He had considerable energy and an ability to focus on what was important. The Franciscan scholar Maynard Geiger describes him as "eager, optimistic, zealous, dynamic, and even adamantine. Strength of character and undeviating purposefulness marked his entire life. (He was) primarily a man of action. He remained a model priest despite his distractions and activities, a man of prayer and mortification."

25

Miguel Jose Serra y Aloran was born in the town of Petra on the island of Majorca on Nov. 24, 1713. He entered the Franciscan order on Sept. 14, 1730 at the age of 16. He chose the name " Junipero," which means "Jester of God."

Serra was an exceptionally able student. He was appointed a lector of philosophy before he was ordained a priest. After his ordination, he was selected for advanced studies at Lullian University, in Palma, the island's principal city, where he was awarded the degree of Doctor of Theology. During the years in Palma (1731-1749,) Serra lived at the Franciscan Convento de San Francisco.

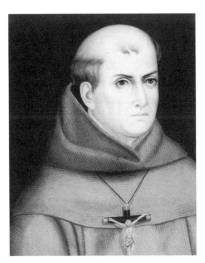

Junipero Serra

Despite his intellectual accomplishments Serra was at heart a man of action, and he yearned to become a missionary. Finally, at 36, he was accepted for missionary service in New Spain.

He left Palma in August 1749 on board the Nuestra Senora de Gaudalupe. His last sight of his homeland was of the massive towers of the 13th century gothic Palma Cathedral, where he preached three times. Serra, arrived at the port of Vera Cruz in December 1749.

Eager to start his missionary training, Serra and another priest decided to walk the 270 miles to Mexico City, rather than wait for a mule train to take them there. During his two-week journey he was bitten on his left foot by a chigger (harvest mite) and the bite became infected. The injury would hamper him the rest of his life.

At the Missionary College of San Fernando, Serra started his one-year missionary training, but within six months he was sent to a struggling mission at Jalpan, in the rugged Sierra Gorda mountains, about 120 miles north of Mexico City.

Serra spent nine years in Sierra Gorda where he had considerable success converting the native Pame Indians. In the mountains Serra pioneered techniques he would later adopt in California. He used drama, stories and a weekly parade through town to attract the natives. He learned the Pame language. He persuaded the college to send livestock and farming tools. Soon the mission had a large neophyte population and became self-sufficient. Work was started on a stone church, completed in 1756. Serra was put in charge of the

Serra Gorda missions, and during his nine years there several additional missions were established.

Serra was recalled to San Fernando College in 1758 where he again taught philosophy and went on preaching tours throughout Mexico. He became known in Mexico City as a fervent preacher. "He would pound his breast with a stone while in the pulpit, or scourge himself," a practice he followed throughout his life.

One contemporary account of a sermon by Serra tells how "Imitating his devout San Francisco Solano, he drew out a chain, and letting his habit fall below his shoulders, after having exhorted his audience to penance, he began to beat himself so cruelly that all the spectators were moved to tears."

Serra spent seven years in Mexico City showing the obedience to his superiors that would mark his life. On several occasions he asked to be allowed to return to return to the field as a simple missionary. Serra's chance came in 1767 when he was selected to head a group of 15 Franciscans being organized to take over the Baja California missions from the Jesuits, whom King Charles III had expelled from New Spain.

At that time, the town of Loreto, on the Baja peninsula, was headquarters for both Baja and Alta California, and Serra became well acquainted with the military governor, Capt. Gaspar de Portola. He worked closely with Portola to organize an expedition to settle Alta California and was selected by San Fernando Missionary College to lead the small initial band of missionaries in the effort. His first recruit was his old friend, Francisco Palou.

During his 15 years in Alta California, Serra returned once (in 1773) to Mexico City for consultation. He was quite sick during his stay and many pleaded with him to stay at San Fernando, but he insisted on returning to Alta California where he served an additional nine years.

Serra died in his room at Mission Carmel on August 28, 1784, at age 71. Toward the end, he had great difficulty breathing and was suffering from tuberculosis. He was buried on August 29 in the floor of the church.

Serra has received considerable recognition for his role as the "founder of California" and for his saintly life. His boyhood home in Petra, where he lived from age 6 to 15, is now a shrine. The Junipero Serra Museum was built in 1929 on Presidio Hill, the original site of the first mission he founded. Statues of Serra abound, at the state capital in Sacramento and, of course at the missions. Serra was selected on March 1, 1931 to represent California in Statuary Hall in Washington, D.C.

The most important recognition of Serra, for the Catholic faithful, would be his canonization (the process by which a person is declared a saint.) The Congregation for Causes of Saints initiated the formal process on August 28, 1934, and it has progressed rapidly. The official investigation of Serra's life was completed in 1949, when he was found to be a "person of impeccable virtue" (a status referred to as fama sanctitatis.) Serra was declared "venerable for sainthood" (the first of three steps) on May 9, 1985. Pope John Paul II declared Serra "Blessed" (Beatification is the second step in the formal process) on Dec. 11, 1987. The official ceremony was held at St. Peter's Basilica on Sept. 25, 1988.

". . . THE WORKS HE PERFORMED when alive shall be impressed in the minds of the dwellers of this New California; despite the ravages of time, they shall not be forgotten . . .

Father Junipero ended his life as subject to Time, having lived 70 years, nine months and four days, (he) labored in the apostolic ministry half of his life, and in these Californias, 16 years . . . leaving behind in Upper California . . . previously inhabited only by pagans . . . 15 settlements.

❦ Francisco Palou, in *Life of Fray Junipero Serra*, 1787

REFERENCES:

Junipero Serra: A Pictorial Biography by Martin J. Morgado. Monterey, CA: Siempre Adelante Publishing, 1991. A richly illustrated and well-researched biography.

Blessed Junipero Serra and the California Missions (http://www.calmissions.org) has a detailed "Timeline Toward Sainthood."

The Man who Founded California by M.N.L. Couve de Murville, Archbishop Emeritus of Birmingham, England. San Francisco, CA: Ignatius Press. A historical and spiritual biography.

Life of Fray Junipero Serra by Francisco Palou, first published in Mexico City in 1787. *Palou's Life of Fray Junipero Serra*, translated and annotated by Maynard J. Geiger, Washington, D.C. Academy of American Franciscan History, 1955. A definitive first-hand source written by Serra's close friend of 40 years.

Franciscan Missionaries in Hispanic California – 1760-1848 by Maynard Geiger, San Marino, CA: The Huntington Library, 1969. Short, candid biographies of all the missionaries who served in Alta California.

History of California, Vol. 1 by Hubert Howe Bancroft, 1884. Contains an extensive discussion of Serra by the noted early historian.

San Gabriel Mission

*When Anza brought the first large group of settlers to California from Mexico in
1775, they stayed initially at the San Gabriel Mission, which became a major
crossroads on the Anza Trail.*

CHAPTER 4

JUAN BAUTISTA de ANZA

Spanish Pathfinder who established the first
overland trail to California in 1775

On Oct. 10, 1775, the vanguard of an expedition destined to bring the first large group of settlers to Alta California reached Tubac, in the Sonora territory of New Spain. Families had been recruited in April and May from poor villages in the Province of Senora, Mexico. They had been specially trained for the arduous trip that would cross hostile Apache territory en route to California.

When the settlers arrived in Tubac, they learned that the Indian threat was real. Three weeks earlier, a band of Apaches had stolen several hundred horses assembled for the expedition, right out from under the noses of the Tubac garrison.

The expedition's ultimate destination was the northernmost section of Alta California – the presidio of San Francisco. The Spanish wanted to settle the area around San Francisco Bay as quickly as possible to thwart further Russian incursion.

The group being assembled was the first party to use a trail intended to supply the missions of Alta California. The trail, laid out the previous year, extended from present day Arizona (the jumping off point would be the presidio of Tubac) to the California mission of San Gabriel (near Los Angeles.) The group would then follow the Kings Highway, El Camino Real, north. The California missions, first established six years earlier in San Diego, had proved difficult to supply by ship. Since the missions were still not self-sufficient, the very survival of the Spanish in California required a reliable land route.

A rising star in the Spanish military, 36-year-old Juan Bautista de Anza, had volunteered to lay out the trail the year before. He actually paid part of the cost himself. Anza was regarded as a brave and effective soldier. He had fought the Apaches continuously since 1766.

Anza started promoting the need for a land route to California in 1772, and had discussed the project with the Viceroy himself. The project was not the ambitious move of a young officer eager to advance. Anza had a deeper motive.

Apaches had killed his father, Juan Bautista de Anza Sr., in 1740 when Anza Jr. was barely 3. Anza's father had talked about the need to discover a trail to the Coast and had done some preliminary exploration in 1737. The trail was an Anza family project.

Based on his credentials and willingness, Anza was authorized to discover the optimum route. He left Tubac in January 1774, arriving back in May, having traveled all the way to the newly established presidio in Monterey. Upon his return Anza was promoted and asked to organize an expedition to colonize San Francisco Bay.

The second Anza expedition was a significant undertaking. There were 300 individuals in the party: Soldiers under the command of Anza and his assistant, Jose Joaquin Moraga; caballeros to shepherd 1,000 head of livestock; muleteers and of, course settlers. The two Franciscans accompanying the expedition were Friar Pedro Font, who was an expert at reading latitudes and Father Francisco Garces, a prominent Franciscan pathfinder. Because of the rough terrain, there were no wagons or carts. All supplies—six tons worth—were loaded on pack mules every morning and unloaded every evening.

The Anza party left Tubac on Oct. 23,1775. Over the course of the next six months there were nine live births and one miscarriage among the women in the expedition. Remarkably, only three people in the party died on the long journey. The expedition arrived at the San Gabriel Mission in Alta California on Jan. 4, 1776. After resting, the party

Juan Bautista de Anza

continued up the coast, arriving in San Luis Obispo in early March, then San Antonio de Padua on March 6-7 and the Carmel Mission on March 11. Advance scouts were in San Francisco by the end of the month.

The members of the Anza party settled the San Francisco Bay area.

Anza himself had another critical assignment, to escort several of the most influential Yuma Indians to Mexico City. He escorted Chief Palma and three other leaders of the Yuma tribe to Mexico City, where they were baptized on Feb. 13, 1777.

Anza continued his illustrious career. He was made commander of all the Spanish troops in Sonora in the fall of 1776, and then promoted to governor of New Mexico, in 1777.

Anza faced his most significant military challenge in 1779 when there was a major uprising by the Comanches under the command of Chief Cuerno Verde. Anza was sent with 800 men and 2,500 horses to conquer the Comanches. He led an expedition across New Mexico and Colorado, cornering the chief near Rye, CO. The peace treaty he signed with the Comanches that year lasted longer than any other treaty signed with that warring tribe.

Over the next few years Anza was called on for the most

ANZA TAKES LEAVE OF SETTLERS

Having concluded my tasks, at 2 in the afternoon I began my return march in company with Father Fray Pedro Font, seven soldiers of my command, because two had gone to notify Commander Rivera and another had remained at the mission of San Gabriel; the commissary who came with the expedition; six muleteers of the expedition, because the rest who came are remaining voluntarily, and four of them I left as deserters and thieves sentenced to work on the fort of San Francisco until his Excellency shall make some other disposition; two of the three cowboys who came, for the other likewise remained here; and four of my servants.

At 2 in the afternoon, then, I set forth over the same road by which I had come. We followed it to the east-southeast for four leagues, for the most part through some hills, from which we descended to the river of Monte Rey, where, in the place that they call Buenavista, at 6 in the afternoon we halted for the night, having traveled three hours and covered four leagues.

This day has been the saddest one experienced by this presidio since its founding. When I mounted my horse in the plaza, the people whom I have led from their fatherlands, to which I am returning, remembering the good or bad treatment which they have experienced at my hands while they have been under my orders, most of them, especially the feminine sex, came to me sobbing with tears, which they declared they were shedding more because of my departure than of their exile, filling me with compassion. They showered me with embraces, best wishes, and praises which I do not merit. But in remembrance of them, and of the gratitude which I feel to all, and the affection which I have had for them ever since I recruited them, and in eulogy of their faithfulness, for up to now I have not seen a single sign of desertion in anyone of those whom I brought to remain in this exile, I may be permitted to record this praise of a people who, as time goes on, will be very useful to the monarchy in whose service they have voluntarily left their relatives and their fatherland, which is all they have to lose.

❦ From the *Diary of Juan Bautista de Anza*, April 14, 1776.

difficult assignments. He led an expedition to Hopi country to help save that people who were dying from a long-term drought. In 1780, he was asked to discover a route between Santa Fe, New Mexico and Arizpe, Sonoma.

In 1787, at his request, Anza retired as the governor of New Mexico. His last known task was conducting a review of the troops at the Tucson Presidio in the fall of 1788.

Juan Bautista de Anza died at his home in Arizpe on Dec. 19, 1788. He is buried in the side chapel of the cathedral at Arizpe.

SAN FRANCISCO BAY

I went to the narrowest opening made by the mouth of the port , where nobody had been before. There I set up a cross, and at its foot I buried under the ground a notice of what I have seen, in order that it may serve as a guide to any vessels that may enter, as well as a report of what I am going on to explore in order to establish the fort belonging to this harbor.

Very soon after leaving the site of our camp I began to find running water, an infinite supply of firewood, timber for barracks, mostly of oak, both green and dry and of good thickness, but bent toward the ground because of the constant northwest winds on this coast. I found a good site for planting crops with irrigation by taking the water from a good spring . . . a little more than half a league to the east of the camp there is a very large lake . . .(where) with a week's labor and with a stockade and an earthen embankment it could be made extremely abundant. . . . on the banks of the lake good gardens can be planted, for it is already known that the climate is good, and that the crops grow with less moisture because of the heavy fogs which fall almost every night, and of the cloudy days, which are many in the course of a year, and even the majority, it may be said.

In the district which I have examined today and from which I returned at five o'clock in the afternoon, I have also encountered numerous and docile heathen, who have accompanied me with great pleasure but without going a step outside of their respective territories, because of the enmity which is common among them.

🦋 From the *Diary of Juan Bautista de Anza* — March 18, 1776

35

Drawing of the San Francisco Presidio. Source: Hubert Hugh Bancroft's *History of California.* Original in collection of Bancroft Library.

Almost all the members of the Anza expedition were born on this continent and had mixed European, African or Indian parentage. Their diverse backgrounds helped shape the history of California.

Anza selected the site for the San Francisco Presidio and 28 soldiers from the expedition were assigned there.

In 1990, U.S. Congress created the Juan Bautista de Anza National Historic Trail, comprising the overland route of the colonizing expedition from Tubac, Arizona to San Francisco, California.

REFERENCES:

Anza's California Expeditions 5 Volumes. Herbert Eugene Bolton, Editor, Berkeley, CA, 1933. The definitive early reference work.

Juan Bautista de Anza National Historic Trail, by Don Garate, Southwest Parks and Monuments Association, 1994.

Anza Conquers the Desert by Richard F. Pourade, Copley Books, 1971. Very readable.

From Sonora to San Francisco Bay: the expeditions of Juan Bautista de Anza, 1774-1776 by John R. Brumgardt. A useful reference.

There are rich resources on Anza and the Anza expedition on the Internet. They include: Web de Anza from the University of Oregon http://anza.uoregon.edu/; Desert USA—Juan Bautista de Anza http://www.desertusa.com/magjan98/jan_pap/du_anza.html

Discoverer's Web http://www.win.tue.nl/~engels/discovery/anza.html

Presidio Days Santa Barbara 2001
Governor Philipe de Neve established the Santa Barbara Presidio in 1782.

CHAPTER 5

PHILIPE de NEVE

The first Civil Governor, who created the
system under which California was governed

After eight years of struggle, Spain's colony in Alta California was in a precarious position in 1777. Conversions were slow. Indians had attacked Mission San Diego in 1775, killing three Spaniards and forcing abandonment of the mission for nine months. San Luis Obispo had been set afire by flaming arrows several times. San Juan Capistrano was temporarily abandoned.

The primitive mission buildings, flimsy structures built of poles and mud, with dry tule thatch roofs, were vulnerable. None of the compounds, for that matter, none of the Spanish presidios, were properly walled. There were only 146 soldiers in all of California most of them ill-equipped and poorly trained.

The fundamental problem was that the eight missions that existed were nowhere near self-sufficient. The missions were still almost totally dependent on supply ships from San Blas, which were often late. Local agricultural production was inadequate. Costs were running far beyond what was allocated from the royal treasury.

Fortunately, in early 1777, the Spanish authorities turned the future of California over to a man who would transform the situation.

Philipe de Neve became the first governor of Alta and Baja California on March 3, 1777. Over the preceding months, he had served as military governor of all of California from a base in Loreto, in Baja. During the period he had limited authority over the "northern annex," but had access to considerable information about the state of affairs in Alta California.

Neve received a copy of a royal decree in July 1776 ordering the capital of the Californias be moved to Monterey. Neve reached Monterey in February 1777, and took full command on March 3, 1777.

Four issues jeopardized Spain's Alta California settlement, according to Neve: An understaffed, poorly trained military; excessive dependence on New Spain for food and supplies; poor communication, particularly linking the north and south; and an unworkable set of rules and procedures under which California was governed. Within months of his arrival he began to address the four issues.

As an experienced soldier, Neve moved immediately to strengthen the military. He ordered compulsory target practice once a week, and saw to it that the soldiers were trained. He refocused the responsibilities of the soldiers posted at each of the missions, relieving them of peripheral tasks such as the care of all the mission horses. He ordered that walls be constructed around the presidios to improve defense and he improved the soldiers equipment and increased the size of the California garrison (by about 25 percent).

Neve also expanded the number and role of settler militia, and encouraged the recruitment of former soldiers as settlers. His most enduring contribution, however, flowed from a broad reorganization of finances and the implementation of streamlined regulations. He reorganized the commissary, removing unjust surcharges on the soldier's pay thereby increasing their take-home real pay.

Neve also took steps to protect the neophytes from his soldiers. He ordered that soldiers of the mission guard not be permitted to enter Indian villages unless accompanying a priest. He disciplined soldiers for consorting with, or abusing, Indian women. His efforts to change the behavior of the soldiers met with only partial success. But under Neve and his Spanish successors, a small contingent of soldiers protected the frontier, helped open up an additional dozen missions and made the system, with all its faults, work.

In order to make the territory more self-sufficient, Neve founded the first "pueblos" in Alta California – free standing

WE MUST MUZZLE OURSELVES and not exasperate the numerous heathendom which surrounds us, conducting ourselves with politeness and respect. Soldiers of the mission guard are not to pass the night away from the mission, even if the Fathers demand it. . . . It is highly useful to the service of the King and the public welfare that the heathen of these establishments do not learn to kill soldiers.

🦋 Neve in *Instruccion*, Sept. 7, 1782

41

towns where each settler had a plot of land and was expected to grow enough crops to support themselves and supply the presidios in the area.

Neve had spotted a promising location for the first town on the east bank of the Guadalupe River in the center of present day Silicon Valley. Rather than wait for settlers to arrive from New Spain (a one- or two-year prospect), Neve recruited nine soldiers with farming experience from the San Francisco and Monterey garrisons, supplementing them with five settlers. He founded San Jose de Guadalupe on Nov. 29, 1777 some nine months after his arrival in California. Within five years, the San Jose Pueblo was supplying the presidios of Monterey and San Francisco with all the corn and produce they required.

There was an even greater need for a center of agricultural production in the south. Neve personally supervised, in

August 1781, the layout of the new town, situated on a broad plain about 12 miles southwest of Mission San Gabriel. What would become California's largest city, El Pueblo de la Reina de los Angeles, was founded on Sept. 4, 1781. It had an initial population of 32.

Over the following decades the presidios would gradually disappear and only a few of the missions would become the centers of new towns. However, the two pueblos Neve founded would flourish, perfectly sited on the most extensive plains in the coastal area of California.

Neve was convinced that he had to find a way to protect land routes between the growing Spanish presence in Southern California and the northern missions. The large landmass northwest of Los Angeles, populated by a "vast heathendom" was a natural barrier. There were no passes through the coastal mountains, and El Camino Real, the primitive dirt road connecting southern and northern missions, was often impassible along the coast in the rainy season. More worrisome to Neve, the narrow road could easily be closed if the Chumash Indians, who populated the area, became hostile.

The answer was clear to Neve who, early in his term as governor, finalized plans for a new presidio and three missions in the land of the Chumash. Again, the New Spain bureaucracy took several years to fund the venture and recruit settlers. The core contingent of soldiers and settlers finally arrived at San Gabriel in late 1781. They were housed in 40 temporary huts during the winter.

Early 1782 Neve led an expedition up the coast, stopping in present day Ventura, where Father Junipero Serra founded Mission San Buenaventura on March 30. Meanwhile, the main party began construction of the presidio, which Neve named Santa Barbara. He personally selected a magnificent site for the future mission, on a hill overlooking the Pacific. Serra dedicated a small temporary chapel at the presidio site in

April. By June, the core buildings were finished and the entire compound was walled.

Neve had a bold plan to reform the mission system, which he planned to start to implement in Santa Barbara. However, the plan put him in conflict with the Franciscans. He was convinced that the current mission system made it unlikely that the Indians would ever be able to function on their own. Neve planned to leave the Chumash Indians in their own villages, where they could be taught to farm, and

Living history interpretation of Neve by Michael Hardwick

"persuaded by teaching and example alone to accept the Catholic faith." Under Neve's plan, the mission itself would be smaller, staffed with only one padre.

When Serra learned of Neve's plans, he refused to supply missionaries for Santa Barbara or La Purisima. These two strong willed men were at an impasse. Neve, convinced that that the system had to change, simply delayed the founding of any more missions until New Spain could rule on the matter.

Neve thought he had the backing of his superiors. His proposed set of new rules and regulations, known as the Neve Reglamento, for governing California, had been approved on Oct. 24, 1781. The Reglamento, adopted almost exactly as Neve had drafted them, established a new basis for financing and governing California. They provided a blueprint for the development of a self-sufficient territory. They also codified Neve's proposed reform of the mission system with several changes that would give the Indians more freedom and lead to an orderly ultimate transfer of mission lands. The Neve

43

Reglamento became the fundamental code governing California through the remainder of the Spanish period. Since this document established the basis of pueblo land titles it remained binding even after the annexation of California in 1848, and was largely upheld in the U.S. courts.

The portion of Neve's regulations that would have changed the mission system itself was never implemented, however, and was formally suspended at the end of 1782. The Franciscans convinced New Spain that weakening their control over the missions was premature and that many of the Neve proposals wouldn't work, (reducing the missionary staff to one priest, for example). Serra had already outmaneuvered Neve in 1778, when a modest step he took to give the Indians more independence, failed.

One can only speculate how the mission system might have evolved if Neve's philosophy, if not the specific form of administration he laid out, had been implemented, and the mission Indians trained for independent living. Rather than move in stages toward more freedom, the system ultimately became more controlling, particularly after the Mexican takeover. Soldiers were increasingly used to recapture runaways, something forbidden by Neve during his tenure as governor.

Neve did not live to see the strategic plan he formulated come to full fruition. Neve had to leave California in the fall of 1782 to command a force being assembled to subdue the Yuma Indians. He was named Commandant General of the Interior Provinces (the second highest position in New Spain) on Feb. 15, 1783, and promoted to the military rank of brigadier general.

Neve, who was not well, requested that he be allowed to retire and return to Spain, but he was considered irreplaceable. His expedition against the Yuma was inconclusive. While on campaign he developed severe dysentery. Tumors developed on his left shoulder and stomach and soon he could neither ride nor walk. He died on August 21, 1784 in the Mexican state of Chihuahua, at age 57. He had not seen his family for 20 years.

REFERENCES:

Filepe de Neve: First Governor of California, by Edwin A. Beilharz, California Historical Society: San Francisco, 1971. The only complete English-language biography. Draws on all of the primary sources.

Franciscan Missionaries in Hispanic California 1769-1848, by Maynard Geiger, San Marino, CA. 1969.

History of California, by Hubert H. Bancroft, San Francisco 1884; seven volumes.

M. PHILIPE DE NEVE, Commander of the Interior Providences of Mexico, who died about four years ago, was a man replete with humanity, and a Christian philosopher. He sought to restrain certain practices (constraint, servitude and punishment of the Indians.) He thought that the progress of the faith would be more rapid and the prayers of the Indians more agreeable to the Supreme Being, if they were not constrained. He was desirous of a constitution less monastic, affording more civil liberty to the Indians, and less despotism in the executive power of the presidios, the government of which might be entrusted to cruel and avaricious men. He thought likewise that it might be necessary to moderate their authority by the appointment of a magistrate, who might be the tribune, as it were, of the Indians, and possess sufficient authority to defend them from vexation.

🦋 Jean Francois, in *Voyages de La Perouse autour du Monde*, published in Paris in 1786

45

Chumash Indians in Plank Canoe

The Chumash Indians occupied a large portion of the California coast north of present day Ventura. One of the most important Chumash Chiefs, Pedro Yanunali, helped the Spanish get established in Santa Barbara.

CHAPTER 6

PEDRO YANUNALI

Chief of the Chumash, who supported the
Spanish presence in Santa Barbara and
ultimately converted to Christianity

The Spanish plan to settle Alta California was simple – on paper. They would establish a presidio and mission at each of the two major ports they had discovered, San Diego and Monterey, then rapidly add other missions in between. Much of the territory in between was the land of the Chumash, who called themselves the First People. The Chumash lived in villages along the California coast, from present day Malibu to the southern edge of Monterey County. A "temi," or chief, headed each large village, or related complex of villages.

One of the most powerful Chumash chiefs was Yanunali, who ruled 13 Indian villages in the Santa Barbara area.

The first Spanish mission, San Diego de Alcala, was founded on July 16, 1769. When Don Gaspar de Portola, the leader of the expedition marched up the coast that August, he stopped at many Chumash villages enroute. Historians believe that Portola met Yanunali, who at that time was the 32-year-old eldest son of the chief.

Throughout the Chumash territory the natives were friendly. They supplied the Spanish with seeds, fruit, fresh fish and meat. The tribe impressed the Spanish. They were artistic and industrious. The positive experience with the Chumash convinced the padres that the natives would be receptive to conversion. The land of the Chumash was given high priority in the planned expansion of the chain. It was fated to be delayed for a dozen years. San Buenaventura, on the southern edge of the Chumash land, was supposed to be the third mission founded, but Indian unrest in the south, a lack of soldiers and other priorities, delayed the founding of this mission until 1782.

It took the leadership of the first civil governor of California, Philipe de Neve to move Chumash settlement back to a high priority. Neve concluded that a presidio and several missions had to be built as quickly as possible to secure the passage between north and south, and strengthen Spanish defenses along the coast. He personally led the expedition that founded San Buenaventura and the Santa Barbara presidio in 1782.

By this time, Yanunali had succeeded his father. When the Spanish arrived to build the presidio they courted the chief aggressively. Michael Hardwick writes, "Yanunali was plied with gifts from Governor Philipe de Neve. The presidio commandante, Francisco Ortega, was instructed to inform Yanunali that the Spanish had come in peace to build a fort and protect everyone from danger, including the Indians who were often the target of raids from marauding Tulares from the great interior valley beyond the mountains."

Chief Yanunali had reservations about the Spanish settlements, fearing they would overtax the available water, but he was persuaded to cooperate. He supplied workmen to help build the presidio. They were paid with beads. Neve left Lt. Jose Francisco Ortega, the first commandant of the Santa Barbara presidio, with 41 bundles of beads to use in his dealings with the Chumash.

Over the next decade many Chumash were converted to Christianity, but Yanunali resisted. After a four-year delay, caused by a disagreement between Neve and Father Junipero Serra over the mission charter, a mission was constructed at

Santa Barbara, about a mile and a half northeast of the presidio. Conversions increased and the Santa Barbara mission soon grew into a large complex that included 250 Indian houses.

House of Pedro Yanunali

Finally, in August 1797, Yanunali was baptized with the Christian name of Pedro. He was 50 years old. He and certain other converts were allowed to continue living in their villages.

Pedro Yanunali would live to see the Spanish presence increase to four presidios and 19 missions, including other missions in the land of the Chumash (La Purisima in 1787 and Santa Inez in 1804).

Who were the Chumash?

The arrival of the Europeans marked the beginning of the end of a remarkable people. Archeologists have found evidence of settled Indian villages in southwestern California that date about 10,000 years ago.

The natives that evolved into the group we know as the Chumash lived in a resource rich environment. The natives lived off the land. They hunted, fished and harvested acorns from the dense oak forests.

In 1769 when the Europeans arrived to settle Alta California, John R. Johnson estimates there were "more than 15,000 Chumash living in villages on the Northern Channel Islands and adjacent mainland. Each village was connected to others through complex social, political and economic ties. There was an extensive trade network that utilized small white shell beads as currency.

The Chumash lived in domed houses. Each significant village had granaries, a ceremonial dance ground, a field for game playing and a village burial ground. Large villages had a temescale, or sweat lodge, for the men.

The Chumash were skilled artisans; particularly noted for their baskets, stone implements and boats. The most unique Chumash boat was a plank canoe called the tomol. The tomol were about 30 feet long and could propel through the water as fast as someone could run. The Chumash were also noted for their rock art, primitive drawings made on rock, usually in remote caves.

The Chumash were a religious people who, according to Gibson, believed "everything on the earth possessed some spiritual power. Therefore religion was part of each daily activity, whether it was collecting seeds, finding rocks for stone tools, or performing ritual dances."

As the Spanish presence spread in Chumash territory, the Indian way of life began to change. Indians converted to

THE WHITE PEOPLE NEVER CARED for land or deer or bear. When we Indians kill meat, we eat it all up. When we dig roots, we make little holes. When we build houses, we make little holes. When we burn grass for grasshoppers, we don't ruin things. We shake down acorns and pine nuts. We don't chop down the trees. We only use dead wood. But the white people plow up the ground, pull up the trees, kill everything. The tree says, "Don't. I am sore. Don't hurt me." But they chop it down and cut it up. The spirit of the land hates them . . .

The Indians never hurt anything, but the white people destroy all. They blast rocks and scatter them on the earth. The rocks say, "Don't. You are hurting me." But the white people pay no attention. When the Indians use rocks, they take little round ones for their cooking. The white people dig deep long tunnels. They make roads. They dig as much as they wish. They don't care how much the ground cries out.

How can the spirits of the earth like the white man? That is why God will upset the world – because it is sore all over.

❧ *The Way We Lived, California Indian Stories, Songs & Reminiscences*, California Historical Society

Christianity had to move into the mission complex, with separate housing for young girls. The number of active Chumash villages declined. In 1782 the last village was abandoned.

According to Phillip Walker and John R. Johnson, who studied Chumash demography in depth, the neophyte population in the five Chumash missions peaked in 1805 at 5,602. By 1834, just after the missions were secularized, the headcount had been reduced to 1,182. The first California state census in 1852 uncovered fewer than 600 Chumash people.

The decline can be traced to several factors. European diseases were a major factor. There was a widespread measles epidemic in 1806; chronic diseases like tuberculosis and syphilis were widespread. Birth rates fell off after Chumash moved to the missions, and infant mortality increased. As the population of the coastal villages declined and word spread of the nature of mission life, conversions plummeted among these free-spirited people. Runaways became a continuous problem. In the Mexican era soldiers were used aggressively to recapture or kill runaway Indians; whippings of Indians increased and an unpaid soldiery became crueler.

Once the friendliest of all Native Americans, there was a serious revolt among the Chumash Indians in 1824. The immediate spark was the flogging of a respected neophyte by a guard at Santa Ines, however, years of cumulative abuse led to an uprising of all the Indians at Santa Ines. In the ensuing melee much of the mission was burned, and two Indians killed. The soldiers sent for reinforcements, but before a contingent could arrive from the Santa Barbara presidio, the rebels fled to La Purisima where the Indians there joined them. The band, now numbering in the hundreds, seized possession of the entire complex, and fortified the grounds. They held the mission for a month. Finally troops from the Monterey garrison crushed the revolt. Seven of the leaders were executed, 18 others whipped and imprisoned, and no effort was made to listen to Indian grievances. It was the beginning of the end.

Yanunali did not live to see the decline of the system he embraced. He died April 4, 1805 at the age of 68. He is buried at Mission Santa Barbara.

A 19th century drawing by Alexander Harmer. Source: Missions and Missionaries of California by Fr. Zephrin Engelhardt

Indian neophytes became skilled at carpentry and iron work, and fabricators of adobe brick at all of the California Missions, where building went on for decades. The Chumash represented by Pedro Yanunali were particularly experienced at woodworking

.

REFERENCES:

Pedro Yanunali 1737-1805, by Michael Hardwick. One of a series of informative, one-page monographs.

The Chumash by Robert O. Gibson, New York: Chelsea House Publishers, 1991. Part of the Indians of North America series. Clearly written and nicely illustrated in 100 compact pages.

See also Sources of Information on the Chumash Indians at http://expange.com/page/chumashother

"The Many Wives of Pedro Yanunali" by Claude Warren, in *Journal of California and Great Basin Anthropology*, Volume 2, 1977.

The Chumash Indians of Southern California by Leif C.W. Landberg, Los Angeles: Southwest Museum, 1965.

Essays in Population History by Sherburne Cook and Woodrow Borah. Vol. 3 Mexico and California, University of California Press, 1987.

"The Decline of the Chumash Indian Population" by Phillip L. Walker and John R. Johnson, Chapter 10 of *In the Wake of Conflict: Biological Responses to Conquest*, Wiley-Liss, Inc., 1984.

Franciscan with Neophyte

This scene appears in a captivating diorama at Mission San Juan Capistrano.

CHAPTER 7

FRANCISCO HERMENEGILDO GARCES

Franciscan pathfinder and martyr

M issionary duty in the California wilderness was quite hazardous, particularly in the early years, when the Spanish were still struggling to get a toehold in this hostile territory. Fr. Luis Jayme was clubbed to death in 1775 when 800 Yunan Indians attacked Mission San Diego.

A particularly dangerous assignment was to be the Franciscan chosen to accompany an expedition into the wilderness. A young priest from Aragon soon became the padre of choice when there was a particularly dangerous and important journey.

Francisco Hermenegildo Garces arrived at the Mission San Xavier del Bac (in present day Tucson, AZ) in 1768.

Garces quickly demonstrated a special talent for relating to the natives, and an eagerness to explore. Fr. Garces lived among the Gila Indian tribes and ministered on his own to them. Even though he was only 30 years old the Indians began referring to him as the "Old Man," an epithet of affection and respect. Convinced that large armed parties couldn't relate effectively to the natives, Garces took long journeys into Indian Territory on his own, including hostile Apache lands. In 1771, he was gone for three months on a missionary exploration that took him to the mouth of the Colorado River. His first-hand reports of Indian life and the nature of this largely unexplored land were sent to the Viceroy of New Spain in Mexico City, and were often reported to the King himself.

Garces special talent was soon to be called upon to support the struggling missions in Alta California. In 1773, frustrated by delays in opening more missions, Junipero Serra (founder of the California missions) made a special trip to the headquarters of New Spain in Mexico City. Serra convinced the authorities that the struggling missions needed to be supplied by a land route from Sonora to the Pacific Coast. Juan Bautista Anza organized the epic trip, which left Tubac on Jan. 2, 1774 with Garces and another friar assigned to the group. It took three months for the Anza party to reach the San Gabriel Mission, about 15 miles from present day Los Angeles.

Garces also accompanied the second Anza expedition, which escorted a large group of settlers to California in 1775. He thus became a central figure in the development of California.

After successfully completing the assignment, Garces convinced authorities to let him explore California.

He set out with two Indian companions on a remarkable seven-month journey through largely un-chartered land. He followed the Colorado River to present-day Needles. He traveled through the Mojave Desert, and was the first white man to discover the Mojave River. He explored what are today the San Fernando and Antelope valleys and the area of Bakersfield, CA. He traveled and mapped the Kern and White rivers. Toward the end of his long journey, Garces lived for a while with the Moqui Indians in northern Arizona, finally arriving back at San Xavier del Bac on Sept. 17, 1776.

Garces kept a diary of his travels and meticulously documented the number of Indians he encountered, the first accurate record of the native populations in these areas. Over his entire trip, including the second Anza expedition, he had contacts with villages and tribes with a population of 24,500 Indians. The entire neophyte population of California in 1776 was under 3,000.

One of the Indians with whom Garces developed a special relationship during the Anza expeditions was the chief of a large Indian village near present day Fort Yuma. The chief asked the Spanish to send Garces, or another Franciscan, back to live with his tribe and educate them on the Christian religion. The Captain General of the Interior Provinces, Theodora de Croix, eager to push out the frontier of Spanish territory, instead ordered that two missions be established in the area. Garces, who knew the Yumans better than any Spaniard, recommended against such a large presence, but he was overruled. Garces and three other missionaries were ordered to Yuma.

Frs. Garces and Barreneche

The Spanish built the two missions: Purisima Concepcion at Fort Yuma and San Pedro at Bicuner. They sent settlers to the area from Tubac, and began to farm the adjacent land. Just as Garces predicted, the Yumans resented the encroachment of settlers on their land.

The natives, who trusted Garces, made it clear to him that they would attack if the Spanish persisted in the expansion of the settlements. However, his reports of danger were minimized.

The Yumans attacked Purisima Concepcion on July 17,1781 in force, while Garces was saying Mass. He and his fellow missionary, Juan Antonio Barreneche, survived the first day of fighting, and took refuge with some friendly Indians. The chief of the Yumans had explicitly ordered that Garces not be harmed, but an eager young buck discovered and killed Garces and his assistant, Padre Barreneche. Their remains were recovered in December. They were finally buried in the Missionary College of Queretaro on July 19, 1794. Garces was 43 years old when he was killed.

Garces's diary has become an essential reference for historians. He is credited with having been the first white man to reach the Grand Canyon from the West. The noted historian Professor Herbert Bolton called him "a far western Daniel Boone in Franciscan garb." He wrote that Garces "manifested his zeal for saving souls both by physical endurance and by religious ministrations . . . [his] human approach was an important factor in his notable success."

The contemporary references to Garces that have survived describe him as a "hardy, generous, warmhearted" man who always approached the Indians in a direct and friendly manner.

The historian John Gavin writes: "Father Garces was a devoted priest; at the end of his life, a martyr. He was a pathfinder worthy of remembrance, an indefatigable traveler, uncomplaining under the stress of hardship, bold under challenge. In sum, he was one of the most attractive and respectable figures in all the early history of the Southwest."

REFERENCES:

Spain in the Southwest: A Narrative History of Colonial New Mexico, Arizona, Texas and California by John L. Kessell. University of Oklahoma Press: Norman, OK, 2002.

Francisco Garces, Pioneer Padre of Kern by Ardis M. Walker Kern County Historic Society: 1946.

Francisco Garces and New Spain's Northwestern Frontier by Scott Jarvis Maughan. Hayden, AZ, 1968.

A Record of Travels in Arizona and California, 1775-76 by Francisco Garces, originally published in 1777. Hardcover edition by J. Howell Books in 1967.

Franciscan Missionaries in Hispanic California: 1769-1848 by Maynard Geiger, O.F.M. Huntington Library, San Marino, CA, 1969.

THIS AREA HAS BEAUTIFUL HILLS, is safe from all danger of flooding, and suitable for building a mission. I called it San Miguel de los Noches. The people, happy at my coming, gave me meat and fish to eat and a sort of caramel cake made from sweetish roots that are plentiful hereabout. While this was going on I was sorry indeed to note that most of the people would not kiss my crucifix because they say that an old man refused to do so. He said that the tobacco and shell beads were good, but the crucifix was bad and he was afraid of it. An example of that sort readily explains why, when a mission is first begun, the scene may change suddenly from great joy and docility to woes and unavoidable disasters.

They told me that the sea was far away and that they caught their fish in big lakes. They have large deerskins, which the Indians from the west come to buy. I met some of the latter, who urged me to come to their land and who did me a good turn by helping to get my mule and my baggage across the river. Although I tried hard with a big stick to find out the depth of the river, I did not succeed because the current bent the stick . . . Sebastian (his Indian guide) told me afterward that he had sounded the depth by tying a big stone to a hitching rope . . . and playing out the entire length.

🐛 From *A Record of Travels in Arizona and California 1775-76* by Francisco Garces first printed in 1777

Mission Carmel

The Carmel Mission church, designed and built by Manual Ruiz, is considered the most beautiful in the entire chain. This early photograph shows the mission before the area around it was developed.

CHAPTER 8

MANUAL RUIZ and ESTEVAN MUNRAS

The architect who designed and built the Mission
Carmel church and the Royal Presidio chapel in
Monterey, and the Spanish artist who created the
stunning interior of the San Miguel Mission Church

A small group of fourth graders standing outside the splendid Carmel church listened attentively. Their teacher, an eager young nun, explained how the mission was founded on June 3, 1770, more than 200 years ago.

The nun explained that the "founder of California," Father Junipero Serra, conducted the first Mass outdoors, under an oak tree that had bells hanging from it. Indians watched from the nearby hills. Some ran when the soldiers fired their muskets at the end of the service. "Over the next month, the Spanish built a fort, and this mission," she added. A young boy with a skeptical look on his face asked, "Where did they get the rocks to build this church in a month, Sister?"

Of course, it wasn't the church they built. The original mission church, made of earth and poles, wasn't even on the same spot. It was located in Monterey right next to the presidio. The location proved to be an awful choice, and Serra scouted the area to find a more suitable site. He picked a isolated hillside in Carmel Valley, surrounded by a fertile plain, "two gunshots" (about 2,500 feet) from the sea." The first "permanent" mission church in Carmel was a small wood chapel enclosed in a palisade for protection.

Most of the mission churches evolved in size, material and splendor. The present Carmel church is the seventh on the site. By the time it was dedicated in 1797, Serra had been dead for a dozen years.

Because Monterey was the site of government for all the Californias (after 1777), and because the Carmel mission was headquarters for the entire chain, the authorities decided that something "special" was required for the final churches at Carmel and at the presidio. Services at the presidio had been held in a converted storeroom until 1776, when a small inadequate adobe chapel was built.

The answer came in 1791 in the person of Manual Ruiz. Ruiz, an architect and master mason from Mexico City, was sent to the remote province to design and build a permanent stone church at Mission Carmel, and a Royal Chapel at the Monterey Presidio. Ruiz recruited neophytes to quarry sandstone rock from the nearby Santa Lucia Mountains. He trained some of the more talented Indians as masons and carvers.

The Royal Chapel at Monterey was completed in four years. It has been in continuous use since 1794.

At the time of Ruiz' arrival, the Presidio was a sizeable compound, with a solid bank of one-story adobe buildings forming a perimeter around a 1,400-foot square. The authorities wanted a stately church built within the walls of the presidio, one that would serve as a focal point for the growing provincial capital.

Ruiz designed a church with beautiful stonework on the facade. A statue of the Virgin of Guadalupe, carved in chalk rock, sits in a nicho at the top. Experts call the Royal Chapel "an architectural triumph." It has the most ornate exterior of all the Spanish churches of Alta California.

Ruiz started work on Mission Carmel before the Royal Chapel was completed, laying the cornerstone in 1793. While there are architectural similarities between the two stone structures, the Carmel church is distinctive, with two bell towers, a Moorish-style dome and an unusual star-shaped window above the front door.

San Carlos Borromeo de Carmelo is considered by many to be the most beautiful of the California missions. As one mission study put it, "The rough-hewn church reflects the design of a master-mason, interpreted to crude perfection by Indian apprentices. In its setting against sea and river, . . . the unequal towers through which the cliff swallows sweep past the full-sized bells, the star window . . . the solid competence of its vaulted ceiling—

Royal Presidio chapel – Monterey

in all these things, it tells the viewer that here stands the work of men with the mind and heart to design with integrity and warmth."

63

Ruiz was not the only talented professional artisan whose name has passed down through the centuries. Father Juan Martin, the head padre at Mission San Miguel for 20 years, began building a new permanent mission church in 1816.

As the church neared completion he contacted a boyhood artist friend from Catalonia, Spain, to see if he could persuade him to come to California and decorate his church. Estevan Munras was living in Peru at the time. Munras agreed to undertake the project as a favor to his old friend and to see this new land of Alta California. He arrived in Monterey in 1820. Over the next two years, he decorated the interior with bright colors that have retained their original purity to this day. Munras trained the local Indians to stencil, using designs he found in books at the mission library. He simulated balconies, doors and archways—painting directly on the walls. He designed and built an elaborate reredo, constructed of wood, cardboard and cloth.

MATERIALS USED TO PAINT THE MISSIONS

The materials for painting were either imported, or found locally. The pigments were almost exclusively mineral in origin, with the exception of black from charcoal or soot, and some blue made from indigo. No colors were made from flowers, contrary to a popular myth, for such tints fade quickly. Reds could be obtained locally from iron ore or cinnabar, though the brilliant vermilion, carmine and orange had to be imported.

Yellows mostly came from ochres, which are found abundantly throughout California. Green came from copper ore, which could be found locally, but it was also imported in the form of verdigris. Both requests and invoices for colors sent appear among mission documents. The colors, which came in the form of powder, would be mixed with some locally obtained medium, such as cactus juice, for use on walls or on furniture painted in tempera. Linseed oil was used for making the more rarely used oil paints. Paint was eventually obtained from the Yankee ships. Although some brushes were ordered in the early years, most probably were made locally of available materials.

❧ From *The Decoration of the California Missions*

On the frieze above the back wall is a triangle with an all-seeing Eye of God blazing above a statue of St. Michael. Practically the entire massive interior of the church (157-feet long by 27-feet wide, and reaching a height of 40 feet) was filled with decorations done by Munras and his assistants.

The interior of San Miguel survives as one of the most authentic and richly decorated churches of Alta California.

Donald Toomey, an expert on Spanish devotional art, noted that the church's interior decorations are "simple, unpretentious and refreshing in their clear proportions and their honesty. . . . who can visit Mission San Miguel and not come away with the lasting remembrance of those painted simulated doorways, archways, huge comb like shells and columns painted on church walls that are totally unaltered by latter day restorers?"

A grand fiesta was held when the church at Mission Carmel was dedicated in 1797. However, the architect of the hour, Ruiz, had already returned to Mexico. He never returned to California.

Munras had to return to Spain for a family emergency in 1821, but he was determined to come back to a land he had come to love and a young lady he was courting. He returned to Alta California in 1822 and married Catalina Manzanelli. He settled in Monterey where he and Catalina had five children. He died in 1853 at age 55.

ARCHITECTURALLY, THE MISSION BUILDINGS as a group represent a very satisfying combination of honest design and simple construction materials and methods.

The padres were not trained engineers or architects, and their building plans incorporated features that they remembered from the churches they had known in Mexico or Spain. The plans were adapted by rule of thumb and harsh necessity to the unique conditions at the outpost. As a rule, the padres could draw upon the services of only a few trained artisans and experienced workmen, and they had to create the building materials out of the soil they stood on and the trees that shaded them.

When they were able to secure a skilled designer, as at Carmel . . . they were able to erect buildings that faintly echoed some of the rich ornamental feeling of the more elaborate structures in Mexico, but even these are bare by comparison

The plain facades of the California missions scarcely prepare the visitor for the richness of decorative detail that he is likely to find when he enters the church. What catches the observant eye is not the gilt, the winking ruby candles, or the figures of the saints . . . but the simple ornamentation applied by artists' hands from another world, trained in another century, and stating their creative message in fresco, stonework, woodcarvings and forged iron.

🦋 From *The California Missions*, Sunset Books: Menlo Park, CA. 1979

Mission Carmel Church today
Source: Photograph by David J. McLaughlin

66

After secularization the splendid church built by Manuel Ruiz slowly deteriorated. Ultimately the roof collapsed and the church was roofless for 30 years. Services were held monthly in the sacristy, which did survive. A temporary roof was put on the church in 1884 and the mission was fully restored in 1936.

REFERENCES:

Migrations project at http://www.migrations.org

The Spell of California's Spanish Colonial Missions by Donald Francis Toomey. An expert on Spanish devotional art, Toomey's book is full of interesting details on Baroque architecture, art and church life in Alta California.

The Decoration of the California Missions by Norman Neuerburg, Bellerophon Books: Santa Barbara, CA. 1989. Generously illustrated with photographs and original drawings, this clearly written 80-page book summarizes the materials and techniques used to decorate the missions; also highlights the distinctive features in each mission.

67

Mission Dolores

The Spanish mission in San Francisco, popularly called Mission Dolores, was completed in 1791. Count Nikolai Rezanov spent time at this mission in 1806.

CHAPTER 9

NIKOLAI PETROVICH REZANOV

The Russian Count who sailed to San Francisco in
1806 seeking supplies, fell in love with the daughter
of the Commandant and died a tragic death in
Siberia on his way home to seek permission to marry.

The seeds of colonial California's greatest love story can be traced to Sitka, Alaska. Czar Paul I granted the Russian-American Co. a 20-year monopoly in 1799 on the Alaska fur trade, and Sitka became the capital of Russian territorial Alaska.

While Sitka ultimately became quite successful, in 1806, the Russian outpost was near starvation. In desperation, the Russians sent a ship, the Juno, to Alta California to obtain supplies. A 42-year-old nobleman, Count Nokolai Petrovich Rezanov, commanded the ship. Rezanov was Imperial Chamberlain at the Russian Court, and a major investor in the Russian-American Co.

The Juno sailed into San Francisco Harbor on April 8, 1806. The Russians were brought to the Presidio, however, communication was next to impossible. The language barrier was overcome when Father Jose Antonio Uria, the presidio's chaplain, started talking in Latin to the ship's doctor, a German named George Heinrich von Langsdorff .

The Russians were treated courteously as guests of Commandante Don Jose Arguello, and invited to stay at his home.

Rezanov hoped to set up a trading arrangement with the Spanish, bartering Sitka furs for grain and provisions. However, he was initially rebuffed. A few days stretched to a week and then a month. In the meantime, the winsome young daughter of the commandante had caught the eye of the count. Maria de la Concepcion Marcela Arguello (usually referred to as Conchita) was an attractive 15-year-old beauty. Langsdorff described her in his journal as "distinguished for her vivacity and cheerfulness, her love-inspiring and brilliant eyes and exceedingly beautiful teeth, her expressive and pleasing features, shapeliness of figure . . . and an artless natural demeanor." Razanov, a bachelor since 1802 when his first wife Anna died, was smitten. The two spent the weeks they had together exploring the presidio and Bay area, and planning a life together at the imperial court.

When Rezanov formally proposed to Conchita her parents were horrified. There was a big difference in religion, in the couple's ages and their daughter, a favorite, would have to live in Russia. Gradually, however, the family came to accept the handsome count. The engagement was approved and a marriage contract drawn. The couple was to be married in San Francisco in two years. Meanwhile, Rezanov would sail back to Sitka to deliver supplies, then make his way to St. Petersburg to gain consent for the marriage from the Czar. He would also obtain approval for the mixed marriage from the Russian Orthodox Church. The Spanish would seek approval of the King and the Pope. By the time the approvals were obtained, Conchita would be at a more suitable age for marriage.

Dr. Langsdorff followed the progress of the affair closely. He noted in his journal "a close bond would be formed for future business intercourse between the Russian American Co. and the provincia of Nueva California." The prospect of a union cleared the way for the Russians to obtain the supplies they sought.

Rezanov left San Francisco on May 24, bound for St. Petersburg. He carried with him a small gold locket containing strands of Conchita's hair—her parting gesture of her enduring love.

During the overland trek through Siberia Rezanov caught pneumonia, but he pushed on anyway. During a relapse he became feverish and fell from his horse, sustaining serious injuries. He died in Krasnoyarsk on March 1, 1807. On his deathbed he asked a young officer to return the gold locket to Conchita and tell her that his final thoughts were of her. Unfortunately, it would be two years before word of Rezanov's death reached his fiancée.

Nikolai Petrovich Rezanov

Conchita waited patiently for Rezanov's return. As she matured she became even more beautiful, and she had many suitors. However, she remained true to Rezanov, and was devastated when word of his death finally reached her.

Conchita never married. She cared for her parents, and did charity work throughout California. Later in her life she entered the convent and became a Dominican nun.

Sister Mary Domenica Arguello (Concepcion de Arguello) died in 1857 at the age of 66. A simple gravestone marked the spot she was buried in St. Dominic's Cemetery on Hillcrest Avenue in Benicia. The Native Sons of the Golden West erected a monument near her grave in 1968.

The Russians continued hunting seals and sea otter in Alaskan waters, pushing further south each year. Sitka became self-sufficient, and for a time, the Russian American Fur Trading Co. was larger and more successful than its chief rival, the Hudson Bay Co. The Russians built a fortified village at Fort Ross in 1812, about 75 miles north of San Francisco. The fear of Russian incursion into Alta California that led the Spanish to settle the area became real.

Fort Ross proved to be unviable, and was ultimately sold in 1841 to John Sutter, who outbid General Mariano Vallejo for the property. Ironically, the discovery that sparked the California gold rush in 1848 was made on a stream that ran by the former Russian property. The United States bought all of Alaska for $7 million in 1867.

The story of the Russian Count and the beautiful Spanish maiden has endured in story and song. Bret Harte immortalized her love for the dashing Russian in a poem "Forgotten Dreams." Harte read the poem at a banquet in San Francisco attended by Concepcion, who was still a Dominican nun. The Russian poet Andre Vaznesensky wrote of her unrelenting love. His poem became the basis of the musical Juno and Avos.

REFERENCES:

"Nokolai Petrovich Rezanov" *The Columbia Electronic Encyclopedia*, 1994. Useful for core facts.

A Presidio Love Story, Website of Presidio of San Francisco, National Park Service, http://www.nps.gov/prsf/history/bios

California's Russian Connection by Harlan Hague, a travel article that summarizes Rezanov's trip to San Francisco, reprinted in: http:///www.softadventure.net/cal-russian.htm

Complete Poems of Bret Harte. Includes his poem on the love affair between Rezanov and Concepcion de Agrugello.

Rezanov by Gertrude F. Atherton, an e*book version of a 1906 classic.

Fur Trade and Exploration: Opening the Far Northwest 1821-1852, by Theodore J Karamanski. Toronto, Ontario: University of British Columbia Press, 1983.

FORGOTTEN DREAMS

Forty years on wall and bastion swept the hollow idle breeze,
Since the Russian eagle fluttered from the California seas;
Forty years on wall and bastion wrought its slow but sure decay,
And St. George's cross was lifted in the port of Monterey;

And the citadel was lighted, and the hall was gaily dressed,
All to honor Sir George Simpson, famous traveler and guest.
Far and near the people gathered to the costly banquet set,
And exchanged congratulations with the English baronet;

Till, the formal speeches ended, and amidst the laugh and wine,
Some one spoke of Concha's lover, heedless of the warning sign.
Quickly then cried Sir George Simpson: "Speak no ill of him, I pray!
He is dead. He died, poor fellow, forty years ago this day;

"Died while speeding home to Russia, falling from a fractious horse.
Left a sweetheart, too, they tell me. Married, I suppose, of course!
"Lives she yet?" A deathlike silence fell on banquet, guests, and hall,
And a trembling figure rising fixed the awestruck gaze of all.

Two black eyes in darkened orbits gleamed beneath the nun's white hood;
Black serge hid the wasted figure, bowed and stricken where it stood.
"Lives she yet?" Sir George repeated. All were hushed as Concha drew
Closer yet her nun's attire. "Señor, pardon, she died, too!"

    ❧ From the much longer ballad *Concepcion de Arguello* by
    Bret Harte

Pirate Attack on Monterey

This painting by Emilio Biggari depicts the 1818 attack on Monterey by the privateer Hipolite Bouchard.

CHAPTER 10

HIPOLITE BOUCHARD

The French privateer sailing under the flag of
Argentina who attacked the coast of California
in 1818, burning the Monterey Presidio and
San Juan Capistrano

The inhabitants of Alta California were nervous about their safety in 1818. Spain was losing a war in Europe, and the Spanish were gradually being driven out of South America. Spanish settlements near the coast were increasingly vulnerable. The ports of Callao, Peru and Guayaquil, Ecuador had been attacked in 1816 and news of the raids filtered back to California. Supply ships now arrived infrequently, and Alta California was largely left to fend for itself.

In an already tense environment, ominous news arrived in the fall. On Oct. 6 an American ship, the Clarion, arrived in Santa Barbara from Hawaii. Her captain, a close friend of the commander of Santa Barbara, Don Jose de la Guerra y Noriega, told the commander that people he had met in Hawaii were planning to attack Spanish settlements in Alta California. Noriega immediately sent word to the governor of Monterey, Pablo Vicente de Sola.

Governor de Sola ordered lookouts to be posted at strategic locations along the coast. The task, like most of the hard work at the missions, fell to Indian neophytes.

For a while it seemed like another false alarm.

The lookouts, placed at 25 locations along the coast, didn't report anything unusual. Then, on Nov. 19, two unknown ships were seen passing offshore from the Presidio of San Francisco, the fort which guarded the northern part of the Spanish territory. These ships were in fact, under the command of Capt. Hipolite Bouchard. The ships were also seen on Nov. 20 by lookouts from the Santa Cruz mission and, that evening, by the lookout at Punta Pinos.

The Spanish were ready to try to repel the invaders, but pitifully undermanned. Governor de Sola could only muster 40 soldiers. He set up a battery of cannons on a hill overlooking the beach, and moved six field guns to the beach itself.

The attacking force was formidable, two heavily armed ships and 350 men. The Spanish had only a few hundred soldiers in all of Alta California, scattered along 650 miles of coastline.

The key to a successful coastal raid is surprise, not only to minimize resistance, but also to prevent the residents from hiding valuables. Bouchard, not aware that his raid had been compromised, planned to sneak the Santa Rosa into the port of Monterey at night, then storm the presidio with 200 men under cover of darkness. Lack of wind delayed the arrival of the boats and the attack was never carried out. Artillery near the beach opened fire on the Santa Rosa at daybreak, with devastating accuracy. The majority of the invading force was trapped.

Then, the tide of battle shifted. The wind rose, allowing the La Argentinia to move closer inshore. Boats rescued the majority of sailors stranded on the Santa Rosa.

The next day Bouchard landed nine boats with about 200 men and four cannons. Faced with a vastly superior force, the Presidio's defenders were ordered to destroy their guns, burn the powder and retreat. Bouchard's forces marched unopposed into Monterey. They found the Presidio empty, except for the town drunk. Bouchard raised the Argentinean flag over the Presidio and his troops started to search for valuables, with little success. Bouchard probably visited the

Royal Presidio Chapel, which was not harmed. However, other buildings in Monterey were burned, and gardens and livestock destroyed.

On Nov. 26, with little loot to show for his trouble, the La Argentina and a hastily repaired Santa Rosa departed Monterey.

The Spanish network along the coast was now on high alert, uncertain where the pirates would strike next. Word spread through the mission chain. Indians were recruited and trained as militia in several missions. Coastal missions were evacuated.

Hipolite Bouchard

Meanwhile Bouchard's ships sailed south. On Dec. 6, Bouchard sailed into the shallow bay of Santa Barbara, and over the next couple days, negotiated an exchange of prisoners. He also promised to discontinue his attacks and stay away from the Alta California coast.

On Dec. 14, Bouchard broke his promise. He anchored off San Juan Capistrano, and sent a messenger to the mission, demanding provisions or he would sack the town. The padre in charge refused. Bouchard then sent his second in command, Peter Corney and 140 men to occupy the mission. They burned the king's storehouse, the soldier's barracks and the governor's house.

In the course of their forays, Corney's men discovered ample stocks of wine and spirits. The next day the invading force returned to the ships with some of the crew so drunk they had to be lashed on to field pieces and dragged to the beach. Six men were lost in the raid. Three of the invading forces were killed and three men deserted during the melee and occupation of San Juan Capistrano.

The La Argentina and Santa Rosa sailed away. The pirate raid on Alta California was over.

THE FIRST DAY

Excellency – I present the superior knowledge of Your Excellency the news about what happened in the presidio of Monterey with two frigates belonging to the rebels from Buenos Ayres . . ..

After doing the wicked things the rebels do by custom, like relieving their rage by shooting the animals they found, because they could not shoot people, they stole whatever they found useful in the midst of the poverty in which these people live. They left on the 25th at night. But first they set the presidio on fire, reducing to ashes the row of houses facing north and three more houses facing south. The construction is all of adobe with walls 16 to 19 feet high and a wooden framework on top to hold the tiles, which all collapsed as the wood burned. . . . We could only save two cannons in working condition.

In the presidio fire we lost some 2,000 pesos in soap, tallow, butter, corn, beans, blankets, cloth, rice and some other things of little value belonging to our soldiers. I lost all my furniture and other things that I need very much.

May God our Lord guard the important life of Your Excellency for many years, which I wish for the good of this province.

🦋 Excerpt from the *Report of Pablo Vicente de Sola, Governor to the Viceroy of New Spain, Don Juan Ruiz de Apedaca.* December 12, 1818

Who was this bold seafarer named Bouchard?

Andre Paul Bouchard was born in 1780 in the south of France, near St. Tropez. He joined the French navy just in time to fight for Napoleon in the Battle of the Nile in 1798, when he was 18. Bouchard, then an ordinary seaman, was captured and repatriated. He re-enlisted, serving in the Caribbean. In 1809, he immigrated to the new world. His first stop was the port of Baltimore in United States, then a center for privateers. Privateers were privately owned ships authorized to carry on maritime warfare (particularly the capture of merchant ships and raiding of enemy ports) by one of the belligerents in a conflict. The men who operated these ships were also called privateers.

Bouchard decided to become a privateer, but he lacked the necessary funds and contacts. South America looked like the most promising spot for an ambitious young man with more experience than money. Around 1810, Bouchard traveled to Buenos Aires, the capital of Argentina and joined the rebellion there. By his third year in Buenos Aires, Bouchard was granted citizenship and married the daughter of a prominent local family.

In 1815, he obtained a privateer's commission and took command of the corvette Halcon in October. Over the next year, Bouchard raided shipping along the Pacific coast. The biggest ship he captured was the Spanish frigate Consecuencia, renamed La Argentina.

Bouchard, by this time a lieutenant commander, was appointed captain of the La Argentina. He set out to sea on July 9, 1817 with a bold plan to sail around the world. He planned to attack Spanish ships in the Philippines.

Bouchard's trip around the world was not very successful. It seems the Spanish had stopped shipping gold and silver from New Spain because of the pirate threat. Bouchard finally captured a brigantine and a schooner off the Philippine coast, but the two captured ships got separated from Bouchard's La Argentina and were never heard from again.

Bouchard decided to continue his voyage around the world, reaching the island of Hawaii on August 18, 1818. Hawaii was then an independent kingdom. Bouchard was astonished to learn that the king owned an Argentinean corvette, the Santa Rosa de Chacabuco. It seems that the crew of this ship had mutinied off the Chilean coast and operated as pirates for a while before sailing to Hawaii where they sold the ship to the king for a pittance. Bouchard bought the ship back and executed at least one of the leaders of the mutiny. Bouchard now had a fleet.

While in Hawaii, Bouchard met Peter Corney, an Englishman, who regaled him with tales of Monterey and its riches. Corney had visited Monterey, the headquarters for the Spanish in Alta California three years earlier.

This time Bouchard acted on his bold plan. He recruited Corney to captain the Santa Rosa, and set sail for Monterey. As privateers, these two ships could raid the coast of California "legally," thanks to the letter of marque he held.

There was just one problem. Bouchard's letter of marque expired, and thus he was technically a pirate. The citizens of California—then and now—consider him a pirate. But an expired marque was no obstacle for a man of action like Bouchard. He rationalized that if he had been able to communicate with the government he would have received an extension, so he proceeded with his plan.

After the raid on Alta California, Bouchard headed for home in early 1819. He wrote a self-serving report of his adventure. Later in his career, Bouchard helped liberate Peru by transporting troops of the Argentine-Chilean Expeditionary Force in 1820, and did some limited privateering as late as 1821. However, his days as a privateer were coming to a close. In October 1821, the government ended its privateering program.

During these years, Bouchard made Peru his home. He never returned to Argentina. In 1829 Bouchard was retired with the rank of captain. In reward for his services the Peruvian government gave Bouchard two ranches, and he spent his last years as a gentleman farmer.

Bouchard faded into obscurity until Jan. 6, 1837 when local papers reported "Navy Captain Hipolito Bouchard, of more than 60 years of age, was suddenly killed by his own slaves two nights ago at seven, for which reason he did not express his last will nor did he receive any sacraments."

Bouchard was estranged from Argentina in the last decade and a half of his life, largely due to a dispute with his financial backers. Despite the conflicts, Argentina considers Bouchard a patriot and hero. In 1962, his remains were moved from Peru to Buenos Aires, and he was interred in the Naval Mausoleum at the cemetery of Chacarita. Several schools and ships have been named after him.

AT EIGHT IN THE MORNING I disembarked one league from the fort, and the same day at 10 the flag of the fatherland was flying at the fort's (the Monterey presidio) mast. The fort had 10 cannons . . . a battery below the fort intended to prevent landings had two cannons of eight, and there were also two mobile field pieces. At 11 the next day I ordered that all the food supplies found in town belonging to the king be sent aboard at once . . . I sailed away on the 29th of the same month. I destroyed the fort, the cannons and the presidio, with the exception of the churches and the American civilians houses.

. . . On the 11th (of December) I sailed toward the Mission San Juan (Capistrano) and anchored in its port on the 16th. The same day I sent the commander of that mission a request for some provisions, to be properly reimbursed, to which he answered by word of mouth, that he had . . . powder and shot to give me. The next day at 4 in the morning I sent 100 men at the command of the First Lt. Don Pedro Corney to take possession of the town, which he did by 10 in the morning. At noon he retreated, burning the entire town and sparing only the church and the houses of the American civilians.

❦ From *the Trip Report of Hipolite Bouchard*, February 10, 1819

REFERENCES:

Breschini, Gary S. Ph.D. *Hipolito Bouchard and the Pirate Raid of 1818*. Monterey County Historical Society: 1996. Available online at http://users.dedot.com/mchs/bouchard.html. A concise, well-written story of the raid.

Harvey, Robert. *Cochrane: The Life and Exploits of a Fighting Captain*. A fast-paced, highly readable biography of a naval hero whose life briefly intersected with Bouchard. Cocharane helped Chile and Brazil win independence. His life was the real-life model for C.S. Forester's Hornblower series and Patrick O'Brien's Jack Aubrey.

Lopez, Crolos. "Hipolito Bouchard: Pirate or Patriot?" *Mains' Haul*, Vol. 36, No. 4 Fall 2000. This long, well-written article appeared in the Journal of the Maritime Museum Association of San Diego. It contains fascinating details on Bouchard's life and his raid on the California coast.

Uhrowczik, Peter. *The Burning of Monterey*. Cyril Books: Los Gatos, California 2001. This comprehensive 166-page book provides considerable detail on the 1818 attack. It contains many useful details on the life of Bouchard. Mr. Uhrowczik cites over fifty sources for his scholarship, including several original manuscripts.

THE MEXICANS

1821-1848

Alta California became an indifferently managed territory of a newly independent Mexico in 1821. The missions, economically self-sufficient, survived intact until they were secularized in 1833-34. The Indians to whom land was distributed were quickly hoodwinked out of their property. Some missions were abandoned; others continued to function in a portion of their original buildings, with the support of a dwindling cadre of mission Indians.

The last decade of Mexican rule was a chaotic time with continuous power struggles. Then, in June 1846, a band of northern California settlers declared California an independent republic, a move opposed by the "Californios." The struggle in California was quickly engulfed in a broader Mexican-American War (1846-48), which concluded with the United States' acquisition of California. A few missions continued to function as parish churches, but the mission system was gone forever.

The central characters during the years of Mexican rule were a varied lot: Dedicated Spanish missionaries who stayed rather than return home; a string of marginally competent and often corrupt government officials; the Indians who resisted increasingly harsh controls; the "Californios" who emerged as the dominant landed classes and the many observant visitors to Alta California, whose diaries and journals have created a rich record of a fascinating time that came and went in generation.

Franciscan missionaries signed contracts agreeing to serve 10 years in Alta California. Most of the senior missionaries in place in 1821 had fulfilled their obligations, men like **Felipe Arroyo de la Cuesta**, who had arrived 13 years earlier. Despite severe arthritis, Fr. Cuesta stayed 20 more years. He and other Spanish missionaries provided the continuity of leadership that enabled the missions to function effectively for another 10-12 years.

During the uncertain early years of Mexican rule one thing became clear; the missions were on their own, required to trade their output for manufactured goods, and forced to support an increasingly bitter, unpaid soldiery, who took out their resentment on the Indians. A serious outbreak of smallpox in the 1820s decimated the native population and scared the neophytes. All of these conditions led to periodic rebellions, usually a few individuals or families running away from a single mission. A gifted Indian leader named **Estanislao** organized a large-scale revolt in 1827. His story is a testimony to the courage and character of the thousands of Indians whose labor made the missions viable enterprises.

The young lieutenant who finally crushed the Indian rebellion in 1829, **Mariano Vallejo**, became Commandant General of California in 1836, and the major power in northern California for the next decade. He was one of the few "Californio" leaders to support American immigration and would play a major role in the ultimate transition to American rule.

During their control of Alta California, Spain discouraged entry to its ports, fearful of a takeover by the major maritime powers of the day – France, Britain and the United States. Under Mexico, California ports became more open, leading to a brisk trade with the missions. A class of merchant, traders, emerged, men like British-born **William Hartnell**, who set up business in 1822, married a local woman and became a Mexican citizen.

As California seaports became more accessible, observant visitors told about the fascinating land in their journals and diaries. French sea captain **Auguste Duhaut-Cilly** visited the coast in 1827-28, and later published his pungent observations. One of the most interesting early visitors came overland. The famous mountain man **Jedediah Strong Smith** visited Southern California in 1826-27, and the journal of his encounters with authorities and his observations about missions he visited provides a priceless record. Perhaps a well-educated deckhand wrote the most famous account of life in Mexican California on a barque that plied the California coast in 1834-35. **Richard Henry Dana's** *Two Years before the Mast* provides a vivid description of the hide trade along the California Coast, and the central role played by the missions in the everyday life of the territory.

It took incredible leadership to keep the mission system intact during the unsettling times before and after secularization. The last great Franciscan leader, **Narciso Duran**, served three times as Father-President of the mission chain, advocating for the rights of Indians and the church from a base at Mission Santa Barbara. Duran and the other struggling missionaries received support from wealthy merchants and landowners, men like **Don Antonio Aguirre**. Aguirre would later help establish the first Catholic diocese in California, and serve as its treasurer.

Distracted by bloody struggles for power and enormous internal issues Mexico sent a succession of officials who ranged from the barely competent to the openly corrupt. The worst by far was the last governor a "Californio" named **Pio Pico** (1845-46). Pico not only continued to make large grants of lands to relatives, friends and supporters, he actually sold many of the remaining church buildings to line his pockets.

The end of the Mexican era came rapidly when a small band of settlers, with covert support from American soldiers conveniently "surveying" in the area, declared California an independent republic in June 1846. A broader U.S.-Mexican War had already broken out in Texas, and in July the U.S. fleet invaded Monterey. American troops moved to occupy the rest of California using several missions as military camps. In the Treaty of Guadalupe Hidalgo Mexico ceded all of California to the United States. The mission era was over.

Alexander Harmer's 19th century drawing of the arrival of the Zacatecan Franciscans in Monterey on January 15, 1833. Source: *Missions and Missionaries of California* by Fr. Zephrin Engelhardt

The Zacatecan Franciscans brought in by the Mexicans were, with some notable exceptions, not the same caliber of religious missionaries as those sent by Spain in the early decades of the mission era.

87

Chapel of Cieneguitas and Kaswa village.

CHAPTER 11

FILIPE ARROYO de la CUESTA

The inspiring and talented Franciscan missionary
who spent 25 years building San Juan Bautista, and
who stayed at his post after the Mexican takeover
ever though crippled with rheumatism

When a 27-year-old Franciscan by the name of Felipe Arroyo de la Cuesta stepped off a Spanish supply ship in Monterey, on August 13, 1808, little did he know that within days he would be asked by Mission President Estivan Tapis to take over the reins of the San Juan Bautista Mission. Described as a "swarthy, broad-shouldered" young man when he arrived in Monterey, de la Cuesta would spend the next 25 years guiding the development of the mission.

Not only did de la Cuesta complete the construction of the church (the only one with three naves), he made the mission economically self-sufficient and baptized more than 2,000 natives during his tenure. He also found time to write a vocabulary and phrase book of the local tribe's (Mutson) language and a series of questions and answers on Christian life in Mutson. Fr. de la Cuesta also built an extensive library at the mission, one of the most diverse libraries in the 21-mission chain, and read every book in it, often making extensive notes in the margins.

In addition to his scholarly pursuits, de la Cuesta found time for music. Visitors to the mission report he had an excellent singing voice. In 1829, the padre acquired a barrel organ, which the Indians loved to have played as evening entertainment.

De la Cuesta was also a mechanical wizard of sorts. He constructed his own water clock and loved to tinker with various mechanical things. In short, he was a man of exceptional talent and great zeal. What makes his accomplishments even more remarkable is that de la Cuesta was crippled with rheumatism by the time he was 40, and often had to be carried on a stretcher to answer a sick call.

THERE ARE DIFFICULTIES ALL AROUND and I am overburdened with cares, which render life wearisome. There is hardly anything of the religious in me, and I scarcely know what to do in these troubling times. I made the vows of a Friar Minor; instead, I must manage the Indians, sow grain, and raise sheep, horses and cows. I must preach, baptize, bury the dead, visit the sick, direct the carts, haul stones, lime etc. These are things incompatible, thorny, bitter, hard and unbearable. They rob me of time, tranquility and my health. I desire with lively anxiety to devote myself to my sacred ministry and to serve the Lord.

>❦ Padre Felipe Arroyo de la Cuesta, In a letter to his friend Jose M. Herrera, August 10, 1826

Despite his health problems, visitors found him cheerful and engaging. British Royal Navy Capt. F.W. Beechey visited the mission in 1826 and found the de la Cuesta "good-natured, cheerful, hospitable, amusing, generous, and a good conversationalist, with a fund of anecdotes and proverbs."

So who was Felipe Arroyo de la Cuesta?

The future priest was born April 29, 1780 at Cubo in the province of Burgos, Old Castile, Spain. He was the son of Matias Arroyo and Isabel de la Cuesta. At the age of 16 he became a Franciscan. After eight years of training he was ordained a priest in 1804, at the age of 24.

Young de la Cuesta volunteered to serve in the American missions that same year and set sail from Cadiz on Sept. 2. He would never see his parents or his homeland again. He

MIssion San Juan Batista

arrived at the port of Vera Cruz, in New Spain in the winter of 1804, and immediately entered San Fernando College, where he received additional training for service in Alta California. He departed for California with two other priests in December 1807, arriving in Monterey in August 1708. He was immediately assigned to the mission at San Juan Bautista.

During de la Cuesta's tenure at San Juan Bautista the mission complex continued to expand through the 1820s. He is said to have been involved in all aspects of the development and day-to-day operations of the mission. Franciscan historian Zephyrin Engelhardt notes de la Cuesta's attention to detail, describing him as "a most methodical man, in everything. Hence his time and means were so arranged that he effected wonders in his line while being a wonderful convert maker." His attention to detail is evident in an anecdote on the interior painting of the church at San Juan Bautista. The story goes that de la Cuesta put the job out to bid, but felt that the proposed rate (75-cents per day) was excessive, so he hired a stranded Boston sailor, Thomas Doak, to do the job for room and board. Doak and Indian assistants painted the reredos and altar in 1818, and they are as bright today as the day they were painted.

A SMALL GROUP OF . . . 142 MISSIONARIES . . . (were the) corps of soldiers of the cross who 200 years ago effected the first triumphs of religion and civilization in what is now the golden state of California. Even the least of them deserves an honorable mention for endeavor if not for accomplishment. California was destined to grow and prosper . . . but never would its condition be as primitive, as rugged, or as difficult as it was in the beginning. Soldier and missionary alike referred to California in colonial days as "this last corner of the earth." To many it seemed exile. Men who made sacrifices and who were dedicated could only accomplish what was accomplished here with the material at hand, and at a disadvantageous distance from civilization. All were pioneers who bore the burden and the heat of the day, as well as the solitude of the night. A number were outstanding. Many were merely successful. All tried, and a few were failures. Each one deserves the niche in history he earned.

✿ Fr. Maynard Geiger in *Franciscan Missionaries in Hispanic California*

De la Cuesta's skill in linguistics contributed a great deal to the growth of San Juan Bautista. He could preach in any of seven Indian dialects. He delighted in the young Indian children and started naming the newborns with persons from antiquity.

Fr. de la Cuesta's health deteriorated after he became afflicted with rheumatism, however, he continued to be active in his mission work. At times he was able to travel, and mission records show he baptized neophytes at Mission Carmel, Mission Santa Clara and Mission Dolores.

In 1833, with secularization imminent, de la Cuesta handed over his mission to a Mexican Franciscan. Now almost totally paralyzed and in a wheelchair, he resided at several area missions before moving to Santa Ines in 1836. De la Cuesta died at age 60 on September 20, 1840.

IT WAS THE CUSTOM AT ALL THE MISSIONS, during the rules of the Franciscan missionaries, to keep the young unmarried Indians separate. The young girls and the young widows at Mission San José occupied a large adobe building, with a yard behind it, enclosed by high adobe walls. In this yard some trees were planted, and a zanja, or water-ditch, supplied a large bathing-pond. The women were kept busy at various occupations, in the building, under the trees, or on the wide porch. They were taught spinning, knitting, the weaving of Indian baskets from grasses, willow rods and roots, and especially, plain sewing. The treatment and occupation of the unmarried women was similar at the other missions. When heathen Indian women came in, or were brought by their friends, or by the soldiers, they were put in these houses, and under the charge of older women, who taught them what to do.

The women, thus separated from the men, could only be courted from outside, through the upper windows facing on the narrow village street.

After an Indian, in his hours of freedom from toil, had declared his affection by a sufficiently long attendance upon a certain window, it was the duty of the woman to tell the father missionary and to declare her decision. If this was favorable, the young man was asked if he was willing to contract marriage with the young woman who had confessed her preference. Sometimes there were several rival suitors, but it was never known that any trouble occurred. After marriage the couple was taken to their home, a hut built for them among the other Indian houses in the village near the mission.

❧ Guadalupe Vallejo, "Recollections of Ranch and Mission Days in Alta California," Published in December, 1890 in *The Century Magazine*

93

REFERENCES:

Franciscan Missionaries in Hispanic California by Maynard Geiger, San Marino, CA: Huntington Library, 1969.

The Franciscans in California by Zephyrin Englehardt, Harbor Springs, MI, 1899.

Mission San Juan Bautista by Zephyrin Engelhardt, Santa Barbara, CA, 1931.

Soldiers Barracks—La Purisima

Up to five soldiers were stationed at each mission. The soldiers sometimes abused their power. Estanislao, a charismatic neophyte, organized a revolt against Spanish rule in 1828.

CHAPTER 12

ESTANISLAO

An exceptional Indian neophyte from Mission
San Jose who led the largest and most successful
revolt against the mission system in 1828.

Mission San Jose was a troublesome spot from the time settlement began in the area. Neophytes escaping from Mission Dolores, in San Francisco, often hid in the San Jose area. Throughout much of its existence, Mission San Jose (founded in 1797) was used as a base for military expeditions against the natives in the interior.

Father Naraciso Duran, who was later to become Father President of all the missions, and Father Buenaventura Fortuny, were assigned to the critical San Jose outpost. They worked together for 27 years to build San Jose into one of the most productive missions in the chain. However, there was always an underlying strain of unrest among the neophytes. Tensions increased after Mexico took over Alta California in 1821.

In late 1827, or early 1828, a San Jose Mission Indian named Estanislao organized the largest neophyte revolt in California. Estanislao was no run-of-the-mill Indian. The few contemporary accounts describe him as "exceptionally bright" and "charismatic." He was a favorite of Duran, and given more freedom and responsibility than his peers, serving as an alcade—effectively a policeman—at the mission. It is not clear what turned Estanislao against the system, but he left San Jose with scores of followers. He set up a base in the San Joaquin Valley, and over the next months organized hun-

Estanislao

dreds of escaped neophytes and free Indians to resist.

The Indians began to find effective leaders in the 1820s. A few of their names are known: Pomponio, Joscolo and Cipriano are mentioned in military accounts. Estanislao, who was from the Miwok tribe, became the most notorious.

Estanislao taught the Indians improved hit-and-run tactics. The Indians would mount an assault, and then retreat into the impenetrable tule swamps. They had few guns, so they used sniper tactics extensively. Estanisla himself was a crack shot. Under Estanislao, the rebels developed elaborate defensive outposts, fortified hills with a system of trenches.

After the first two excursions failed, the government decided to mount an offensive. In 1828, the governor called on a capable young lieutenant, Mariano Vallejo, to mount a serious campaign against the troublesome Indians and the leader he would describe in his memoirs as "a real genius." Vallejo, who was later to be made Commandante General of all the troops in Alta California, organized a large force of cavalry, foot soldiers and several cannon. He invaded the Indian territory in May and met considerable resistance.

Vallejo battled Estanislao's band for three days. After several unsuccessful frontal assaults, he set the chaparral on fire, and then led a successful flanking attack.

Lt. Vallejo executed several of the captured Indian leaders, but an extensive search failed to find Estanislao, who had escaped. He turned up a few days later at Mission San Jose, seeking the protection of Duran.

Although hostilities in the area did ease for a while during the 1840s, Indians continued to harass settlers at the San Jose Pueblo.

INDIAN RUNAWAYS

The Indians were friendly and for some years seem to have entered the missions willingly. Once baptized, the Indians were referred to as neophytes, or new converts, yet in fact, they were little better than slaves in spirit and in body. During the mission period the death toll was exorbitant. . . . While the labor demanded of the Indians in the mission was steady, it does not seem to have been unduly harsh. The Indians, however, were by their old custom, unused to steady work all day every day, and when they malingered they were usually punished with the lash at the order of the priest.

Many neophytes found life in the mission unbearable. Those brought into the mission from native villages felt their loss of freedom and self-expression. Presumably those born in the mission learned, as they grew up, to accommodate to the regimen. For individuals who found mission life intolerable because of culture shock, the scarcity of food, the death of family members or punishment for minor infractions, the maximum response was to run away. Fugitives were a source of concern . . . regarded as apostates, or defectors, and were not tolerated because the missionary fathers felt they had failed in their sacred duty to convert and civilize the heathen. Whenever possible the small body of soldiers attached to each mission was sent out to round up and return the runaways. Mission records show that about 10 percent of all neophytes became permanent fugitives. The number of temporary runaways . . . was far greater.

🌺 From *The Natural World of the California Indians*

The fundamental problem facing the missions in 1820s was the lack of Indians to maintain the agricultural lands, extensive cattle ranches and workshops. As the general Indian population declined, and the few unconverted Indians remaining moved inland, the prospect for maintaining the neophyte census through new conversions became a problem. As Sherburne Cook pointed out in his landmark research, many unconverted "wild" Indians were "caught in the net" when military expeditions were sent to find and return runaways. Sometimes the other Indians were released, but "the temptation was strong to baptize them and retain them as neophytes . . . until at end of the mission period, all pretense of voluntary conversion was discarded and expeditions to the interior were frankly for the purpose of military subjugation and forceful conversion."

It was a sad end to a noble race. Many of the California Indians were peace-loving people, with no tradition of organized warfare. The tribes that did resist the Spanish found that arrows and spears were no match for firearms. The California Indians were also fragmented into scores of tribes, unaccustomed to working together for any cause. Until the emergence of a few leaders like Estanislao, the Indians were rarely able to mass enough warriors to really be a threat.

Estanislao himself stayed at Mission San Jose for the rest of his life. Mission San Jose was secularized in 1834, and gradually fell into disrepair. Estanislao died in 1836. Stanislaus County, in California, is named after the Indian leader.

MANY OF THE MISSIONS have been restored often, with a high level of scholarly involvement. Many of the architectural and artistic details are amazingly exact. The human details, however, are invariably omitted: The sight of men and women in irons, the sound of the whip, the misery of the Indians. Without acknowledging the pain and agony that were a major part of mission life, today's carefully restored missions do not portray history. Rather, in the manner of theme parks, they use the ornaments of history to create a soothing world of fantasy.

> ❧ *Life in a California Mission: The Journals of Jean Francois de la Perouse* (1786)

REFERENCES:

General Vallejo and the Advent of the Americans by Alan Rosenus. This book summarizes Vallejo's battle with Estanislao when he was a young soldier.

California Indians: An Illustrated Guide by George Emanuels, Walnut Creek, CA 1990. This book contains a chapter on the Coast Miwok.

The Natural World of the California Indians by Robert F. Heizer and Albert B. Elsasser, University of California Press: Berkeley, CA 1980.

The Conflict Between the California Indian and White Civilization by Sherburne F. Cook, University of California Press: Berkeley, CA, 1976. Re-publication of papers written in 1930s. Drawing on the research of Bancroft and Engelhardt, original mission records, memoirs and the ethnographic work of A.L. Kroeber, these controversial papers brought a new perspective to the impact of the white man and the Spanish missions on Native Americans.

PUNISHMENT OF INDIANS

For the minor faults committed by the Indians, pertaining to the nature of those in the category of faults that might be punished by the father of a family, the padres themselves were authorized to inflict the punishment. They had the right, if they considered it necessary, to call upon the escort for aid (the escort generally composed of a corporal and four soldiers . . . at each mission . . . but at San Gabriel there was usually a larger force.). Serious faults or crimes came under the authority of the district to which the mission belonged. It was the duty of the priest in charge of the mission to investigate the case, arrest the person of the culprit and then inform the commandant of the presidio of the affair.

I do not know what was the greatest number of blows that a father could order to be given to an Indian, but I believe it could not be more than 25. I do not know if the fathers sometimes exceeded or abused their correctional authority, but I do know that they frequently punished the Indians, who gave reason for it, with flogging and imprisonment, and by putting them in irons. On several occasions I saw Indians working shackled, or in the stocks.

> ❦ *Reminiscences on Mission Life* by Jose del Carmen Lugo, who dictated them to Berkeley historian Hubert Howe Bancroft in 1878

99

Mission San Francisco Solano before Restoration

General Mariano Vallejo was the most powerful man in Northern California in the last decade and a half of Mexican rule. In 1834 he was named commissioner for Mission Solano, when the mission was secularized.

CHAPTER 13

MARIANO GUADALUPE VALLEJO

The soldier statesman who controlled Sonoma
and northern California during Mexican rule
and facilitated the takeover of California by the
Americans in 1846-48

The padres at Mission San Franciso Solano in present day Sonoma, in 1834, discovered that most of their cherished grape vines appeared to have been stolen. They soon learned that these critical plantings had been moved "for safekeeping" to Rancho Petaluma, a massive cattle ranch and farmland owned by Mariano Vallejo. The plantings were never returned.

Mariano Vallejo was the most powerful man in northern California during the final years of the mission era. Vallejo was a noted soldier, the man who in 1829 crushed the revolt of Miwok Indians, led by Estanislao, a rebel neophyte. In 1833, after he had attained the rank of colonel, Vallejo established the first military outpost in Sonoma. To help him colonize the area he was given title to what ultimately became a 66,000-acre grant known as Rancho Petaluma.

In 1836 the 29-year old Vallejo became Commandant General of California. Known forever after as General Vallejo, his bold seizure of the Sonoma Mission vines illustrates all the essential aspects of the character of this remarkable man.

Vallejo was a careful forward thinker. He had arranged to be appointed overseer of the Sonoma mission, so he had the authority. Second, the man described as "50 years ahead of his countrymen in intelligence and enterprise," anticipated that with secularization, the mission land would quickly disappear into private hands, which is what happened all over California in the following years. He did "save" the plantings and helped start the California wine industry. Vallejo thus became one of the first commercial winegrowers in California. Of course, on everything from vine transfer to the disposition of mission lands, Vallejo took care of himself and his friends. But in Sonoma the transitions were managed and Vallejo represented a pillar of stability in an increasingly unstable political environment.

Vallejo was a study in contradictions. As one of the most powerful "Californios," the general had the most to lose if one of the major maritime powers took over Alta California. But— always the independent thinker—Vallejo concluded that California could not survive as a territory of Mexico, and actively supported American immigration, an unpopular stance. Vallejo favored American rather than British or French takeover even though a democratic America probably wouldn't be as friendly to him. While he exploited the Indians as laborers on his ranches he respected the Indian way of life, and became close friends with the Suisan Chief Sonoma, the most powerful Indian in what is now Sonoma and Napa. The General Vallejo that appropriated the mission vines personally paid for all the furnishings in the Mission Sonoma church, and protected the integrity of the core of the mission.

The history of the Vallejo family in California illustrates the best and the worst of the Spanish who settled this frontier. His father, Ignatio Vallejo, studied for the priesthood in Jalisco, New Spain (present day Mexico) but soon abandoned his vocation and became a soldier. He arrived in Alta California in 1774, served as an escort to Junipero Serra in the founding of Mission Dolores. He was a competent soldier, but never progressed beyond the rank of sergeant, largely because he was hot tempered and promiscuous. The Spanish soldiers often acted as if the exploitation of Indian women was a right of conquest, but Sgt. Vallejo was particularly flagrant, and the colonial records show he was severely admonished by the governor. Sgt. Vallejo finally settled down, marrying the 14-year-old daughter of a friend. His marriage, which lasted 40 years, was a success, and produced 13 children.

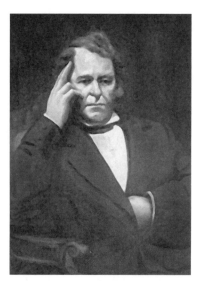

Mariano Guadalupe Vallejo

Mariano Guadalupe Vallejo was born on July 4, 1807, the eighth child and third son of Ignatio and Maria Antonia Vallejo. He was baptized at the Royal Presidio Chapel in Monterey the next day.

Young Mariano grew up at the Presidio in Monterey, where his father worked as a soldier- engineer.

Monterey was a small settlement with a population of about 300 in the early 1800s. This was still an awesome natural environment. The author Alan Rosenas states that "cougars, bear and antelope could be seen from the presidio walls" and "migrating birds were so abundant they literally darkened the skies for hours on end. The skeletons of whales . . . and other ocean dwellers were piled up on the beaches in enormous shell middens . . . indicating the presence of the Costanoan Indians along the shoreline for thousands of years." Monterey was a laid back community whose principal entertainment was horse racing, gambling , fandango dancing and church pageants.

The most exciting thing, which happened to young Mariano, was the invasion of Monterey by the pirate Hipolite Bouchard in 1818. Sgt. Vallejo and his eldest son, Jose de Jesus, were part of the contingent that fought the intruders.

Eleven-year-old Mariano, along with his brothers and sisters, fled with other settlers to the inland Mission Soledad, sleeping that night on blankets provided by the local padre. The pirates stayed in Monterey a week and destroyed most of the presidio.

Mariano Vallejo closest friends were Juan Bautista Alvarado (a future governor of California) and Jose Castro (a future commandant general.) The governor took a shine to these three exceptionally bright boys and made sure they received the best education possible. Mariano himself was tutored by William Hartnell, a British hide and tallow trader who taught Vallejo English, French and Latin. For a while Vallejo worked for Hartnell as a clerk. In 1822, when he was still only 15, Vallejo became secretary to the governor and was present when news was received that Mexico had won its independence from Spain. The official acknowledgement of the transfer of allegiance from Spain to Mexico was written in his script.

Mariano Vallejo was enrolled as a cadet in the Monterey company in 1824, and was soon promoted to corporal. By the time he was 20, Vallejo was a second lieutenant. In 1833 Jose Figueroa was made governor of California, and he took an instant liking to the capable young soldier who was then serving as military commandant of the San Francisco presidio. Newly married with a young son, Vallejo received a plum assignment that was to be the basis of his fortune. He was to reconnoiter the area North of San Francisco and find a good site to station soldiers, to create an additional buffer zone between the Californians and the Russians, who had built a settlement at Ft. Ross. Vallejo recommended that soldiers be posted to Sonoma, the site of Mission San Francisco de Solano.

Vallejo was sent to establish a military presence and begin to colonize this area. Vallejo set to work immediately to expand the small community. He laid out a grand square for the town and built soldiers barracks on one corner, near the

Mission quadrangle. In June 1835 he was named Director of Colonization of the Northern Frontier. In that role he encouraged Americans to settle in California.

Vallejo had complete control of Sonoma and the surrounding area from the mid-1830s on. He built a two-story adobe on the north side of the Sonoma plaza. When it became clear California would not survive as a province of Mexico, Vallejo argued for union with the United States.

Vallejo was a central actor in the American takeover of California. He was captured and imprisoned for two months at Fort Sutter during the so-called Bear Flag Revolution in

IT IS MOST TRUE, that to rely any longer upon Mexico to govern and defend us would be idle and absurd. . . . It is also true that we possess a noble country, every way calculated, from position and resources, to become great and powerful. For that very reason, I would not have here a mere dependency upon a foreign monarchy, naturally alien, or at least indifferent, to our interests and our welfare. . . . Although others speak lightly of a form of government, as a freeman, I cannot do so. We are republicans – badly governed and badly situated as we are – still we are all, in sentiment, republicans. Why then should we hesitate still to assert our independence? We have indeed taken the first step, by electing our own governor, but another remains to be taken, annexation to the United States. In contemplating this consummation of our destiny, I feel nothing but pleasure, and I ask you to share it. Discard old prejudices, disregard old customs, and prepare for a glorious change, which awaits our country. Why should we go abroad for protection when this great nation is our adjoining neighbor? When we join our fortunes to hers, we shall not become subjects, but fellow-citizens, possessing all the rights of the people of the United States and choosing our own federal and local rulers. We shall have a stable government and just laws. California will grow strong and flourish, and her people will be prosperous, happy and free.

🦋 Speech given by General Mariano Vallejo in early1846, when the future of California was being hotly debated.

105

1846, when a band of settlers declared California an independent republic. After California was formally ceded to the United States in 1848, Vallejo helped in the transition. He moved from the center of Sonoma to a less prominent location outside town in 1850 where he built a deliberately non-Spanish style house, called Lachryma Montis, now a part of the Sonoma State Park.

Vallejo's later years had their ups and downs. Court battles to retain his land drained much of his wealth. However, he was rarely bitter and advised his son, "We are in the United States, soon to be the foremost nation on earth. Love everybody. Be good. Obey just laws. Let be . . . I brought (my current troubles) upon myself. I did what I thought was best. It was best for the country and so far as I am concerned, I can stand it."

In his advancing years Vallejo did much to preserve memories of the California that was no more. He devoted considerable time to helping the historian Hubert Howe Bancroft collect original records and interview old-timers. He helped artists like Oriana Day document the old missions. He was generous with his dwindling funds. He purchased the papers of William Howell from Howell's widow when no one else wanted them, in order to help the wife of his old tutor.

Years ahead of his time as always, Vallejo last venture and primary source of income in his waning years was the sale of fresh spring water from his property to the citizens of Sonoma.

Mariano Guadalupe Vallejo died on Jan. 18, 1890 at his home, Lachryma Montis. He was widely honored as one of the original builders of California and "America's friend." In 1921 there was a poll taken in northern California to decide which two individuals from the ranks of California's illustrious dead should be honored with niches in the National Hall of Statuary in Washington, D.C. Junipero Serra was chosen . . . in second place, after General Mariano Vallejo.

AUSTRALIA sent us a swarm of bandits who on their arrival in California dedicated themselves exclusively to robbery and assault.

France, desiring to be rid of several thousand lying men and corrupt women, embarked them at the expense of the government on ships, which brought them to San Francisco.

Italy sent us musicians and gardeners. The former, of course, lost no time in fraternizing with the keepers of gambling houses and brothels, while the latter, poor but industrious folk, settled in huts and dark caves near the mission. They cultivated gardens, raised poultry, and in a short time, became rich since vegetables brought fabulous prices from '48 to '53, and eggs sold from $6 to $12 a dozen.

Chile sent us many laborers who were very useful and contributed a lot to the development of the resources of the country. Their favorite occupations were woodcutting and farm labor.

China poured upon our shores clouds and more clouds of Asiatic and more Asiatic. The Chinese, without exception, came to California with the determination to use any means of enriching themselves . . . and returning to their own country.

But all these evils became negligible in comparison with the swollen torrent of shysters who came from Missouri and other states of the Union. No sooner had they arrived than they assumed the title of attorney and began to seek means of depriving the Californians of their farms and other properties. The escaped bandits from Australia stole our cattle and our horses, but these legal thieves . . . took from us our lands and our houses, and without the least scruple, enthroned themselves in our homes like so many powerful kings.

🦋 Mariano Vallejo in "What the Gold Rush Brought to California"—Date uncertain, probably late 1850s.

Mariano Vallejo's house, Lachryma Montis.
Source: Photograph by David J. McLaughlin

Vallejo's two-story Gothic-style home, located on a 20-acre estate about a half-mile northwest of the Plaza, is now a State park. It stands at the end of a long lane bordered by shade trees. A former storehouse Vallejo used to hold wines, olives and other produce is now a museum.

The site had abundant spings. General Vallejo translated the Indian name for this location into Latin. Lachryma Montis means 'Tears of the Mountains.'

REFERENCES:

General Vallejo and the Advent of the Americans by Alan Rosenus. Berkeley, CA: Heyday Books, 1995. An illuminating, well researched biography.

Historical and Personal Memoirs Relating to Alta California (5 volumes) by Mariano Vallejo, Bancroft Library at the University of California, Berkeley, CA. The results of Vallejo's extensive collaboration with Hubert Bancroft.

Vallejo: A California Legend, by Alexander Hunter. Sonoma, CA: Sonoma State Historic Park Association, 1992.

Indian Women

William Hartnell, an early hide and tallow merchant, was named Visitator General of the Missions in 1839. he vigorously defended the rights of the natives during his tenure. This mural is on the wall of the San Luis Obispo museum.

CHAPTER 14

WILLIAM EDWARD PETTY HARTNELL

One of the early hide and tallow traders who became a Mexican citizen, protected the missions and founded the first school of higher education in California

After the Mexican government secularized in the missions in 1833-34, mission lands were systematically taken over by "Californios," many of them relatives and friends of local officials. The Indians, who were supposed to be the primary beneficiaries of the secularization, were cheated out of their land. Some wound up working on the vast ranches that emerged, others moved inland to try to recreate an easier life. However, at most of the former missions, a surviving core of neophytes struggled to survive.

The Mexican government created the position of Visitator General to try to exert some degree of central control over the administration of the vast holdings and protect the Indians. However, the first incumbents in the position were political cronies who used their roles to enrich themselves and their friends.

William Hartnell, an early British hide and tallow merchant, who had lived in California since 1822, was appointed Visitator General in 1839. He worked hard to negotiate more fair land distributions and protect Indian rights. He dismissed corrupt local mission administrators, including an influential Mexican named Pio Pico, who controlled the Mission San Luis Rey holdings.

The Mexican power brokers moved to stop Hartnell. General Mariano Vallejo imprisoned Hartnell for a time when he came to inspect Mission San Francisco Solano. Soon there were threats against Hartnell's life and he was forced to resign his position in September 1840. A few years later Pico took his personal revenge on Hartnell when he became governor, stripping Hartnell of all the government licenses and privileges he had accumulated over two decades, and barring him from any government position.

So who was William Hartnell?

He was born on April 24, 1798 in the county of Lancashire, England. He started calling himself William Edward Petty Hartnell to honor his uncle, who became his guardian when he was 17, after his own father died. His uncle arranged a job for him as a bookkeeper in the firm of John Begg & Company in Peru in 1819. He helped open up a branch office in Lima. There, Hartnell met Hugh McCulloch. The two young men decided to become partners and enter the hide and tallow trade in California. They called their firm Macula and Arnel, which was easier for Spanish-speakers to pronounce.

Hartnell and his partner arrived in Monterey in 1822, two months after California became a territory of Mexico. There were only 13 "foreigners" in Alta California at the time, and it was not easy for someone who was neither Spanish nor Catholic to become accepted.

Hartnell had an easy-going manner that won over the governor, Pablo Vicente Sola, who granted the partnership the right to do business and live in California. The partners set out to obtain contracts with the primary source of hides and tallow, the missions. Hartnell, the better negotiator of the two, was able to obtain contracts from all but two of the northern missions.

Macula and Arnel soon won permission to trade in any port along the California coast – a significant advantage over rivals who were often restricted to one port.

I BELIEVE YOU ARE ALREADY INFORMED of my being taken into partnership with my late employers, jointly with my former fellow clerk Mr. H. McCulloch, and of our destination to this country for the purpose of forming an establishment for the collection of hides for the Europeans and tallow for the Lima markets.

We have now been here about 15 months and have every prospect of succeeding in our undertaking. We have already had four vessels to our consignment, have sold two valuable ships' cargos and are at present loading two vessels; one with hides for England (which will be the first cargo of the description ever procured in this country and the only vessel that ever sailed direct from New California to Europe), the other with tallow for Lima. The firm here is McCulloch, Hartnell & Co.

New California consists of four presidios, 19 missions, and two small villages. Monterey is the capital . . . the missions, which are inhabited almost entirely by Indians, are under the direction of the friars of the order of Saint Francisco, who are in general jolly, fat, good-natured fellows, who do nothing all day but pray and fill their bellies.

We have been fortunate enough to induce the greater part of them to enter into a contract with us for all the hides and tallow that the missions may produce for the ensuing three years, which circumstances give us great advantage over any other person who might be tempted to come here and set up in opposition to us.

I beg your acceptance of the accompanying bow and arrows. They are the only curiosity this out of the way place affords.

. . . I remain, Dear Uncle, yours very affectionately.

❧ Letter of William Hartnell to his uncle, Edward Petty, on July 10, 1823

113

Shortly, McCulloch returned to South America and Hartnell was left to build the business.

Hartnell's business flourished, but he became depressed when he learned of the business failure of his favorite uncle. Hartnell, with the support of Father Luis Martinez, converted to Catholicism. Martinez is credited with building San Luis

Obispo into one of the most successful missions in the chain. Hartnell was baptized on Oct. 13, 1824 at Mission Carmel. In 1825, Hartnell married Maria Teresa de la Guerra, a 16-year old beauty whose father was an influential man in Santa Barbara. Over a 25-year marriage the Hartnells had 19 children.

After a few years of success, the hide and tallow business became increasingly competitive. Hartnell gradually diversified his business activities with help from his father-in-law. Hartnell became a citizen of Mexico in 1830, since citizenship was required to own land. He acquired property in present day Salinas, where he built an adobe house. He called his ranch El Patrocinio de San Jose.

WILLIAM HARTNELL . . . created a plane of understanding in a primitive, diverse community and presided over it for many years. By the end of his life, Monterey had become a microcosm, a little world inhabited by people from many countries. Each stranger was assured of welcome and understanding at La Casa Arnel (Hartnell's home.) Only discourteous conduct ever barred the door.

Hartnell played the undramatic, indispensable role of interpreter throughout his life. Procedures at California's constitutional convention might have ground to a standstill, without Hartnell's contribution, his ability to explain and reconcile clashing convictions. Instead, it became one of the most successful conferences in history. Hartnell spent the last years of his life translating new laws so all who must obey them could understand them. The first school of higher learning and liberal arts, the first girls' school and the inception of public education in California – all these we owe (to Hartnell.) Through stern effort, he helped to bridge from war to peace, to conduct his conquered country out of chaos into order. He educated his own and other children for enlightened citizenship, girls as well as boys, Indians along with Anglos. And he loved his wife so deeply and enduringly that she was sustained for the time she must spend on earth without him.

❧ Susanna Bryant Dakin in *The Lives of William Hartnell*

Hartnell was a hospitable, friendly person. He opened his house to foreign visitors, including British Capt. Frederick Beechy, who stayed with Hartnell in 1827. He built a grandstand on his property so that guests, family and friends could watch rodeos.

Hartnell opened one of the first schools in California on Dec. 10, 1833. It was not a success and closed after less than two years.

William Edward Petty Hartnell

Hartnell began to work for the government to supplement income from his ranching. When Juan Bautista Alvarado became governor of California in 1836, Hartnell's fortunes improved. Hartnell had tutored Alvarado as a young man. Alvarado was also a cousin of Hartnell's wife, Teresa. Connections meant a lot in colonial California and Alvarado named Hartnell commissary treasurer, tax collector and customs administrator of Monterey. Hartnell did well until 1845 when the man he had crossed as Inspector of the Missions, Pio Pico, became governor, and took his revenge. Hartnell was saved from financial ruin with the help of his wife's family.

By 1846-47 all the major powers were maneuvering to take over California. Hartnell hoped that Britain, the country of his birth, would prevail, but soon concluded that a union with the United States was inevitable.

Hartnell assisted U.S. Navy Commodore John Sloat, who sailed into Monterey Harbor in late 1846, to translate a proclamation into Spanish. He also translated all the Mexican laws into English, a yearlong endeavor. When the California constitution was enacted by the first state convention, Hartnell prepared a Spanish version, thus ensuring that California was a bilingual state. He worked for the U.S. government for a time as a surveyor and appraiser.

Hartnell died at age 56 on February 2, 1854.

History has honored Hartnell for his role in establishing the first school of higher education in the state of California. The school was located six miles east of modern day Salinas. Salinas Junior College was renamed Hartnell College in 1948 to honor William Edward Petty Hartnell.

A BULLFIGHT IN CALIFORNIA is far different from the brutal exhibitions of Spain and Mexico. Here, the bull is not killed or lacerated, the object of the amusement being merely the exhibition of equestrian performances. All the young bachelors are expected to be present, which generally secures a full attendance of ladies, who stand on stages and platforms erected around the enclosure, ready to bestow their smiles and approbation on those of their choice; hence the waving of handkerchiefs and shawls is incessant.

When a bull enters, he usually rushes in as if ready to attack anything before him, till the shouts of the multitude and the confused fluttering of scarfs, shawls and ribbons disconcert the animal, and he retires to the least occupied part of the square, where he remains pawing up the earth. Presently, a horseman comes forth, with a scarlet cloak . . . which he waves toward the bull; then the animal rushes at the object, and the skill of the rider consists avoiding a collision. Sometimes a dozen riders are thus in the area at once, and in the confusion, it not infrequently happens, that a horse is gored or a rider thrown. The more valiant appear on foot; and if they nimbly escape danger, or boldly throw themselves into it, the interest is exceedingly increased. When one bull is worn out with fatigue, another is let in to take his place, and occasionally a rocket or squib is thrown to excite his fury. The boys, on horseback, await to receive the harassed creature as he is let out, to drive him off outside the town . . ..

❦ Alfred Robinson, *Life in California*

REFERENCES:

The Lives of William Hartnell by Susanna Bryant Dakin. Stanford University Press, 1949.

A Biographical Study of William Hartnell, A Prominent Californian by Shirley Sales Johnsen. San Luis Obispo: California State Polytechnic College, 1965.

William Hartnell: The Hero and His Colleges by Sean F. Roney http://users.dedot.com/mchs/hartnell2.html

The Diary and Copybooks of William E.P. Hartnell, Gurcke, Starr Pait, transl., and Glenn J. Ferris, ed., Santa Clara and Spokane: The California Mission Studies Association and The Arthur H. Clark Company, 2004.

View from Ruins of Mission Mill

Mission Santa Ines had a grist mill and fulling mill (for the treatment of wool). During his extended stay (1826-27), Captain Duhaut-Cilly visited and traded with most of the missions.

CHAPTER 15

AUGUSTE DUHAUT-CILLY

A French sea captain who visited California in
1827-28, and documented his observations in
a published journal

A French trading ship lay off the coast of California in January 1827, entrapped for eight days in a dense fog. On January 26, the fog lifted, and the Heros sailed into "the great harbor of San Francisco" passing "an old Spanish fort." The master of the Heros, Captain Auguste Duhaut-Cilly, would spend most of the next two years sailing the coast of both Baja and Alta California, and trading with the missions that dotted the coast. On his way home, Duhaut-Cilly recorded his impressions in a diary that offers candid first-hand accounts of the missions and Alta California under Mexican rule.

THE PRESIDIO OF SANTA BARBARA, like that of Monterey, is a square enclosure surrounded by houses and other structures, all of one story. Near the northeast corner is a building somewhat different from the others and surmounted by a small tower; this is the residence of the commandant. In the opposite corner, turning toward the shore road, it is apparent that the California engineers have tried to construct a defensive bastion, but one would have to endow with much charity to call it a success.

❧ Capt. Auguste Duhaut-Cilly, 1827

Auguste Duhaut-Cilly

Duhaut-Cilly's diary describes the missions as they existed in 1827-28: "The mission of San Carlos is built on a small bay, open to the southwest, which offers neither shelter nor anchorage. It is poor and almost depopulated of Indians." **Makes keen observations**: "It was a time of the grain harvest, a time of joy in the fields of France, but no sentiment of this kind was visible on the faces of the Indians occupied in this work." **Sizes up individuals**: "This missionary was an educated man who read much. But whether he chose the most melancholy of books, or had eyes only for the most gloomy passages, he seemed no longer to perceive the world except through a funereal mist." **Describes the system**: "The Californians themselves do not work the fields; for this they obtain Indians and pay wages to the missionaries." **Discusses religion**: "A Californian thinks himself a good Catholic when he conforms to the exterior marks of devotion, although he pays no attention to what religious demands or prohibits." It is no wonder than historians have treasured this candid first-hand account.

Who was Duhaut-Cilly?

Duhaut-Cilly was born in March 1770 in Saint-Malo, on the coast of Brittany. He grew up in a prominent family that de-emphasized its noble origins after the French Revolution. At 16, young Duhaut-Cilly enlisted in the French navy. As a teenager, he took part in a number of sea battles. After the end of hostilities between the French and English in 1814, Duhaut-Cilly transferred to the merchant marine, ultimately commanding several ships on voyages to the West Indies and South America.

He became captain of the trading ship Heros in 1826 at the age of 56, and embarked on a four-year around-the-world voyage he would chronicle in his diary A *Voyage to California, the Sandwich Islands and Around the World in the years 1826-29.*

Duhaut-Cilly was a well-educated man, fluent in French, Spanish and English. He was also an artist by avocation. Four lithographs of his sketches were included when his diary was first published in two-parts, in 1833-34.

> ON THE EVE OF OUR DEPARTURE (from San Francisco), I received from Don Ignacio Martinez, an official letter in which he asked me, in the name of the Mexican government, to convey (on board our ship) to San Diego, three bad Indian subjects whom he had to keep in irons to prevent them from escaping and robbing the people of the presidio and the mission. Since it was to my advantage to maintain good relations with the agents of the government, and in spite of my reluctance to support slavery, I consented to the commandant's request. I thought, moreover, that a stay on board would be for these unfortunates, a momentary alleviation of their state, and hoping that a change of location and of masters might enable them to find a better way of life.
>
> ♥ Capt. Auguste Duhaut-Cilly, 1827

121

Above all, Duhaut-Cilly was a keen observer, whose detailed observations about the California missions provide an invaluable first-hand account of the missions near the peak of their development. He also provides insight into the way things really worked.

After his voyage, Duhaut-Cilly appears to have retired from the sea. Duhaut-Cilly broke his collarbone in a fall from his horse in San Diego, and suffered ill health much of the rest of his life. For the next 20 years, the retired captain lived in Saint-Servan, next to the town of his birth, and was for a brief time, mayor of the town. He and his wife, Elise, had six children, none of whom seem to have left any direct descendants. Duhaut-Cilly died of cholera in 1849 at age 79.

Duhaut-Cilly had unusual access to the Spanish missions of Alta California. He traded with most of the coastal missions for almost two years. The captain also visited all of the presidios and pueblos during his stay. As a Catholic fluent in Spanish, he gained the confidence of the missionaries.

His blunt, opinioned account surely would have angered all. He found the Californians "indolent," "vain" and "supersensitive," although they do "excel in everything that has to do with riding." He concluded that the Indians were exploited at most of the missions, but described the "savages" in most unflattering terms ("the women are short, fat and ugly.") He decried the fact that "day by day the (native) traditions are vanishing and being lost." While he admired the missionaries, he found the padres unsanitary and complacent in a system "that can not long endure."

The mission era was over by the time Duhart-Cilly's diary was published, just as he predicted. However, his diary helps subsequent generations understand the pastoral society of Alta California and the missions as they really functioned.

REFERENCES:

A Voyage to California, the Sandwich Islands, and Around the World in the Years 1826-1829 by Auguste Duhaut-Cilly, Berkeley, CA. University of California Press. 1999.

French Explorers in the Pacific in the Nineteenth Century by John Dunmore. Oxford. 1969.

WE WENT UP A FLIGHT OF SEVERAL STEPS, leading us under a long peristyle or cloister, supported by 15 square pillars forming 14 arches which, from a distance, gave the mission (Santa Barbara) the noble look that had struck us at first sight. Here was seated an old and feeble padre, whom age and infirmity had made so insensible to everything around him that he scarcely knew us for strangers when we greeted him and inquired of his health. It would take strong means to get his attention, I could see, and I leaned over him and said, in a tone to vanquish his deafness, "I am French. I have come from Paris and I can give you recent news of Spain."

No talisman ever produced a more magical effect that these few words, whose power to gain the friendly interest of these good fathers I had already experienced. Most Spaniards are strongly attached to their country; they love its land, its customs, everything, even the abuses of its government. No sooner had I pronounced the words that the old man, starting out of his lethargy, so overwhelmed me with gratitude and with urgent questions that I could scarcely find an instant to reply. He had regained some of his lost vigor in speaking of the native land that he would never see again.

123

🦋 Capt. Duhaut-Cilly on his encounter with Father Antonio Jayme, a missionary at Mission Soledad, who had retired to Santa Barbara. He died in 1829, two years after the discussion.

San Luis Rey Mission

Jedediah Smith, an American mountain man, visited Alta California in 1826. In his diary he described the San Luis Rey Mission as "beautifully situated."

CHAPTER 16

JEDEDIAH STRONG SMITH

The legendary mountain man who was the first
American to visit Alta California by land in
1826-27

The only surviving image of Jedediah Strong Smith,
one of the legendary mountain men who opened up
the West, shows a man with an unnatural looking
head of hair. Seven years earlier, when Smith was leading a
party through the Black Hills, he was severely mauled by a
grizzly bear that tore off his scalp. After killing the bear, Smith
ordered his men to sew the dangling scalp back on. Smith
recovered, but his hair didn't.

Smith was the first American to travel overland to California on a southwestern route, through the Mojave Desert. He
was the only trapper to leave a written record of his impressions of the Spanish missions and the country of California.

Most mountain men were rough, illiterate adventurers,
who cursed, smoked and drank heavily. Smith was a quiet
man who shunned tobacco and liquor. He was very religious.
He had been well educated in Bainbridge, N.Y., where he was
born on Jan. 6, 1799. As a youth, he read the riveting report
of the 1804-06 Oregon expedition of Meriweather Lewis and
William Clark. Their adventures captivated Smith and he
resolved to explore the West himself.

Smith was only 23 when he signed up as a hunter with
Gen. William H. Ashley. He proved himself in a fierce firefight
the group had with the Arikaras tribe, near Yellowstone in

1822. Although the youngest man in Ashley's company, within a year, Smith was promoted to captain. He led trapping parties throughout the West over the next several years. After countless adventures, Smith bought out Ashley in 1826, and formed the partnership of Smith, Jackson & Sublette.

Smith and his partners met on the Bear River in Idaho, on August 7, 1826, and decided to split up to "prosecute our business advantageously." Smith, and "18 persons besides myself," made their way to California following old Indian routes, stopping at many of the spots noted by the Franciscan pathfinder Father Francisco Garces four decades earlier.

He entered California after a hazardous trip through the Mojave Desert. It is quite likely he stayed overnight en route at San Antonio Creek, a resting point of the Anza party in 1775-76.

As he entered the territory of Alta California, Smith was apprehensive about his reception by the Spanish, "a people of different religion from mine and possessing a full share of . . . bigotry and disregard of the rights of a Protestant." He was also concerned that the Mexicans would consider him a spy and imprison the Americans.

However, after the bleakness of the Mojave Desert, Smith and his men were glad to be in the "fertile and well-watered valley (with) herds of cattle and bands of wild horses sniffing the wind and rushing wildly across our way." Soon they passed a creek where "a number of Indians were at work." The Indians stopped and "gazed" then "gazed again, considering us no doubt as strange objects." They "were not accustomed to see white men . . . on horses packed . . . with fur traps, saddlebags, guns and blankets."

Smith had arrived at Rancho de la Puente, an outpost of Mission San Gabriel. It was late November. The Americans were received hospitably. At the request of the farm overseer, Smith wrote a note to the "Father" and a swift horse was sent to notify the mission of the stranger's arrival. In about an hour, a corporal from the mission garrison arrived with a note from Father Jose Sanchez, the head Franciscan. It was written in Latin, and Smith observes in his journal, "as I could not read his Latin, nor he my English, it seemed we were not likely to become general correspondents."

The corporal then escorted Smith and his party to the mission.

The Father sent for an interpreter, who turned out to be

ON APPROACHING MISSION SAN GABRIEL

I rode toward a gate that appears quite common in this country, passing large fields laid out on both sides of the road. The fields were fenced with posts set in the ground with rails tied to them by means of strong pieces of raw hide. There were thousands of cattle skulls in rows on each side of the road conveying the idea that we were approaching an immense slaughter yard.

We arrived in at a building of ancient appearance. Not knowing why I was brought there, or who I was to see, the current of my thoughts ran so rapidly through my mind as to deprive me of the power of coming to any conclusion. When we passed in front of the building the corporal pointed to an old man sitting in the portico, and then left. I was left quite embarrassed, hardly knowing how to introduce myself. Observing this, the father took me by the hand and quite familiarly asked me to take a walk, making at the same time many inquiries. Soon some bread and cheese were brought in and some rum of which I drank to please the Father, but much against my own taste.

❦ Jedediah Smith, 1826

127

Joseph Chapman. Chapman was a former American member of the crew of privateers who attacked Monterey in 1818. He was captured during the attack on San Juan Capistrano and elected to stay in California.

While he waited, Smith thoroughly examined San Gabriel. He was impressed by the "great fertility of the soil" where

"2,000 acres of land are fenced, watered by a small creek . . . and produce an abundance of wheat, beans, peas and some corn." He admired the mission's extensive vineyard and "orchards of apples, peaches, pears and olive trees, some figs and a beautiful grove of about 400 orange trees."

Smith was surprised to discover that the young Indian boys, who had guided his party across the mountains, "fine, honest and well-disposed boys of about 16 years of age" had been arrested and charged with being "runaways" from the mission. He surmised that he too was likely to be arrested.

Smith stayed at San Gabriel to await the arrival of instructions from the authorities.

Finally, on Dec. 8, the corporal received orders to bring Smith to San Diego to meet with Governor Jose Maria de Echeandia. The travelers eventually reached San Louis Rey, which Smith describes as "beautifully situated on a rising piece of ground between two small creeks. The buildings appeared better from having been lately whitewashed."

After staying overnight at the mission, they rode to San Diego. Smith was informed that the governor could not see him until the next day. Smith toured the presidio and was appalled by its run-down condition. The town of San Diego had about 200 inhabitants at this time.

Over the next few days Smith didn't get any straight answers from the governor. The authorities asked to examine his journal and questioned why he needed to make maps of "their country." He was detained "day after day and week after week . . . harassed by numerous and contradictory delays."

In early January there was an end to the impasse. The governor informed Smith that "if the Americans who were in the harbor of San Diego . . . would sign a paper certifying that what I have stated as the reason of my coming was substantially correct, I would be given permission to trade for such things as I wanted," but would then have to "leave immediately using the same route by which I had come in." The documents were signed and Smith was given a passport and the license needed to purchase supplies.

Jedediah Strong Smith

The governor refused to provide Smith with horses for the return journey. Capt. John Cunninghim was about to sail up the coast to collect hides, and he offered to drop Smith off at San Pedro. Smith finally reached Mission San Gabriel on Jan. 10, where Father José Sanchez, reinforcing the favorable impression Smith had of the priest, gave him a "cordial welcome." Smith's passport required that he leave the country promptly. He spent several days assembling supplies for the return trip, buying horses in Los Angeles.

129

Smith left San Gabriel on Jan. 27. Once Smith was well beyond San Gabriel's ranches, he headed north, ignoring the governor's stipulation. The Smith party trapped the American River near Sacramento, then Smith crossed the Sierra Nevada with two of his men and rendezvoused with his partners in the Salt Lake area.

Smith retraced his journey to Southern California in late 1827, but this time disaster struck. While he was crossing the Colorado River, Mojave Indians attacked his party, killing more than half of his men. The eight survivors made their way to California, where the Mexicans jailed Smith for a while. He then traveled up the central coast of California where he undoubtedly had some contact with the missions, but no written records have survived. After wintering in the San Francisco Bay area, Smith started up the coast to Oregon.

Smith was one of four survivors of an attack on his camp by Kelawtset Indians.

Smith continued to trap and explore the following couple years, but his heart was no longer in it. He had lost many of his friends. His mother had died while he was away. He had had enough of mountain life. Smith and his partners sold their business in 1830 to the Rocky Mountain Fur Co. Smith bought a farm near St. Louis.

Smith had promised the new owners that he would help them obtain supplies and get organized during their first year of operation. Always a man of his word, he left home in the spring of 1831 to fulfill the obligation. While he was on the Santa Fe Trail, crossing the Cimarron River, he was killed by Comanches. Smith was 32-years-old at the time of his death, and his body was never found.

REFERENCES:

The Southwest Expedition of Jedediah S. Smith: His Personal Account of the Journey in California, 1826-1827. Edited by George R. Brooks, University of Nebraska Press: Lincoln, NE, 1977.

"Captain Jedediah Strong Smith, A Eulogy of That Most Romantic and Pious of Mountain Men, First American to Land into California" by James Hall in *Illinois Mountain Magazine*, XXII, June 1832.

Jedediah Smith and the Opening of the West, by Dale L. Morgan, Indianapolis, 1953.

WILD HORSES

We had passed many herds of cattle belonging to the residents of the Angel village (Los Angeles) and thousands of wild horses. The wild horses are so abundant at times as to eat the grass quite clean. My guide informed me that the inhabitants of the village, and of the vicinity, collect horses whenever they consider the country overstocked, and build a large and strong pen with a small entrance and two wings extending from the entrance some distance to the right and left. Then mounting their swiftest horses they scour the country, surround large bands and drive them into the enclosures by the hundreds.

They will perhaps lasso a few of the handsomest and take them out of the pack. A horse selected in this manner is immediately thrown down and . . . blindfolded, saddled and haltered (the Californians always commence with the halter). The horse is then allowed to get up and the man mounts it. When he is firmly fixed in his seat, and the halter is in his hand, an assistant takes off the blindfold. The several men on horseback with handkerchiefs to frighten, and some with whips to whip, raise the yell and away they go.

The poor horse, having been severely punished and frightened, does not think of flouncing, but dashes off at no slow rate for a trial of his speed. After running until he is exhausted, and finding he cannot get rid of his enemies, he gives up. He is then kept tied for two or three days saddled and rode occasionally, and if he proves docile, he is tied by the neck to a tame horse until he becomes attached to the company and then turned loose.

🦋 Jedediah Smith, 1836

131

Hides Curing in Sun

In his best seller *Two Years Before the Mast*, Richard Henry Dana writes extensively about the "hide trade."

CHAPTER 17

RICHARD HENRY DANA

The author of *Two Years Before the Mast,* who
visited Alta California as a young sailor in
1834-35

As the young sailor stared at the coast of Alta California for the first time in early 1834, he found himself "at the ends of the earth; on a coast almost solitary; in a country where there is neither law nor gospel."

This 19-year-old lad, and his shipmates on the barque Pilgrim, would spend the next year in California, trading Eastern goods for hides harvested at the old Spanish missions. Whenever the young sailor had a shore leave, he would have a drink or two with his shipmates, then slip away quietly to explore a land unimaginably different from his native Boston. He explored all the crumbling presidios that "guarded" the coast in San Francisco, Monterey, Santa Barbara and San Diego. He enjoyed a spirited horse race and participated in the extensive festivities that followed the wedding of a prominent local couple. He spent time wandering in the port of San Pedro, and chatting with the men who processed the hides he and crewmates hauled down from the cliffs near the coastal missions. He watched a Fandango in "the Pueblo de los Angeles – the largest town in California." And every night when others were asleep the young deckhand, Richard Henry Dana, made notes of the day's events in a journal.

The old missions, which had just been secularized, feature prominently in this journal. Dana admired the large garden "filled with the best fruits of the climate" at Mission San Diego. He found the Santa Barbara mission "a large and deserted-looking place, the out-buildings going to ruin and everything giving one the impression of decayed grandeur." Dana thought Mission San Juan Capistrano "the only romantic spot in California."

California was thinly settled in 1834, and many of the missions still isolated. Dana tells of the hard climb to the top of the cliffs in present day Orange County, where the country "stretched out for miles as far as the eye could reach . . . the only habitation in sight (being) the small white mission of San Juan Capistrano, with a few Indian huts about it."

The author of this journal was no ordinary sailor, although he had the good sense to hide his privileged background from his shipmates.

Richard Henry Dana was born on August 1, 1813 into a prominent New England family of jurists.

Before his voyage on the Pilgrim, Dana had completed almost three years of college at Harvard when a case of measles weakened his eyes. The doctors ordered him to take a sea voyage.

He was offered free passage to Calcutta through family connections, but instead decided to sign on as an ordinary seaman on one of the trading ships that plied the Pacific Coast.

His ship, the Pilgrim, was an 86-foot long barque, small for the dangerous trip around Cape Horn. The owners, Bryant and Sturgis, thought the Pilgrim would be ideal for collecting hides, which could then be stockpiled and processed in the port of San Pedro for ultimate shipment back East on one of the company's larger vessels. The Pilgrim's stay was thus extended, and Dana wound up returning to Boston to resume his schooling in 1836 on another Boston based ship, the Alert, again as a deckhand.

The sea trunk containing Dana's journal disappeared when he disembarked in Boston Harbor, but he reconstructed an account of the trip from memory, using a small notebook and letters home to jog his memory. He published his journal in 1841 titling it *Two Years Before the Mast.* This grand tale – a seafaring classic and compelling coming-of-age story – sold well on its merits, then became a best seller when gold was discovered in California in 1849. *Two Years Before the Mast* was the only first hand English-language account of a land thousands suddenly wanted to reach.

Richard Henry Dana

In 1946 Dana's book was made into a movie starring Brian Donlevy, Alan Ladd and William Bendix.

After returning from his grand adventure, Dana graduated from Harvard with the class of 1837. Following the family tradition he then attended Harvard law school, specializing in maritime law. He became a leader of the American bar, a member of the Massachusetts legislature and prominent expert on admiralty law. He was a life-long advocate of the rights of the merchant seamen he had come to know on the Pilgrim, and more than once helped one of his former shipmates. After publication of his famous account of life at sea, his only other substantive publication was a handbook, *The Seaman's Friend.*

Dana revisited the West Coast for the first time in 24 years in 1859. San Francisco was now a large city and most of the missions in crumbled ruins. Dana spent several months in a nostalgic visit, traveling down to San Diego on a steamer. He summarized his impressions in later editions of his book with a new chapter entitled "Twenty-Four Years After." His retrospective is a rather sad story. Over the course of his travels Dana realizes that "progress" has changed most of the places he cherished in his memories. More fundamentally his early years in California take on a new meaning. He had always dismissed *Two Years before the Mast* as "a boy's book" and "a parenthesis in my life." But in California he discovers no one cares about the subtleties of maritime law, but they have all read *Two Years before the Mast* and loved it. Dana is feted from San Francisco to San Diego. One suspects that this prominent lawyer begins to realize that his enduring life work really took place decades earlier when he was an eager lad hauling hides down the slopes near the California missions. In an unguarded moment he once said he had "been lucky in travel and not much else."

Dana never visited California again. He continued to practice law. Abraham Lincoln appointed him a U.S. District Attorney for Massachusetts. In that capacity he argued and won a celebrated case before the U.S. Supreme Court. The case of the Amy Warwick established the right of the federal government to blockade Confederate ports without giving the Confederate States international status as belligerents. In 1867-68 Dana served as a U.S. counsel in the trial of Confederate President Jefferson Davis.

Despite these prominent accomplishments Dana experienced many disappointments and frustrations in the last years of his life. He was never successful in entering Congress, a lifelong dream. His nomination as ambassador to Great Britain was defeated in the Senate. He became embroiled in a plagiarism lawsuit.

Dana retired from his law practice in 1878, intending to write a definitive book on international law, one of his specialties. To complete his research he moved with his family to Rome in 1881. He contracted pneumonia there and died in early 1882. He is buried in Rome's Protestant Cemetery

(the same cemetery that contains the remains of Keats and Shelley.)

One hopes that at the end he was able to recall that day long ago when he had "the delightful sensation of being in the open air, with birds singing around me, and escaped from the labor and strict rule of a vesse—of being once more in my life, though only for a day, my own master."

COLLECTING HIDES

After a few days, finding the trade beginning to slacken, we hove our anchor up, set our topsails, ran the stars and stripes up to the peak, fired a gun, which was returned from the presidio, and left the little town astern, running out of the bay, and bearing down the coast again, for Santa Barbara. As we drew near the islands off Santa Barbara, (the wind) died away a little, but we came-to at our old anchoring-ground in less than 30 hours from the time of leaving Monterey.

Here everything was pretty much as we left it, the large bay without a vessel in it, the surf roaring and rolling in upon the beach, the white mission, the dark town and the high treeless mountains. We lay here about a fortnight, employed in landing goods and taking off hides, occasionally, when the surf was not high; but there did not appear to be one-half the business doing here that there was in Monterey. In fact, so far as we were concerned, the town might almost as well have been in the middle of the Cordilleras. Occasionally we landed a few goods, which were taken away by Indians in large, clumsy ox-carts, with the yoke on the ox's neck instead of under it, and with small solid wheels.

A few hides were brought down, which we carried off in the California style. This we had now got pretty well accustomed to; and hardened to also; for it does require a little hardening even to the toughest. The hides are always brought down dry, or they would not be received. When they are taken from the animal, they have holes cut in the ends, and are staked out, and thus dried in the sun without shrinking. They are then doubled once, lengthwise, with the hair side usually in, and sent down, upon mules or in carts, and piled above high-water mark; and then we take them upon our heads, one at a time, or two. If they are small, we wade out with them and throw them into the boat, which as there are no wharves, we are usually kept anchored by a small kedge, or keelek, just outside, of the surf.

The great art is in getting them on the head. We had to take them from the ground, and as they were often very heavy, and as wide as the arms could stretch and easily taken by the wind, we used to have some trouble with them. I have often been laughed at myself, and joined in laughing at others, pitching themselves down in the sand, trying to swing a large hide upon their heads, or nearly blown over with one in a little gust of wind. The captain made it harder for us, by telling us that it was "California fashion" to carry two on the head at a time; and as he insisted upon it, and we did not wish to be outdone by other vessels, we carried two for the first few months; but after falling in with a few other "hide-draggers," and finding that they carried only one at a time, we "knocked off" the extra one, and thus made our duty somewhat easier.

After we had got our heads used to the weight, and had learned the true California style of tossing a hide, we could carry off 200 or 300 in a short time, without much trouble; but it was always wet work, and, if the beach was stony, bad for our feet; for we, of course, always went barefooted on this duty, as no shoes could stand such constant wetting with salt water. Then, too, we had a long pull of three miles, with a loaded boat, which often took a couple of hours.

We all provided ourselves with thick Scotch caps, which would be soft to the head, and at the same time protect it; for we soon found that however it might look or feel at first, the "head-work" was the only system for California. For besides that the seas, breaking high, often obliged us to carry the hides so, in order to keep them dry, we found that, as they were very large and heavy, and nearly as stiff as boards, it was the only way that we could carry them with any convenience to ourselves. Some of the crew tried other expedients, saying that they looked too much like West India Negroes; but they all came to it at last.

🦋 Richard Henry Dana in Chapter XIV of *Two Years before the Mast*

REFERENCES:

Two Years Before the Mast by Richard Dana is available online at the Library of Congress website.

Richard Henry Dana by Robert I. Gale, Twayne: New York, 1969. A comprehensive biography, currently out of print, but available at many libraries.

Harvard Magazine published a biography of Dana by Castle Freeman Jr., a summary of which is available online at:
http://harvardmagazine.com/issues/ma89/vita.html

Mission Santa Barbara—1890

Mission Santa Barbara was never abandoned. In the late 19th century the monks were still working the open fields around the mission.

CHAPTER 18

NARCISO DURAN

The last great leader of the mission chain, who
kept the mission network functioning after
their 1833 secularization by Mexico

A young Franciscan arrived at Mission San Jose in July
1806, fresh off the supply ship La Princesa. He was
described as being "tall, with dark hair, blue eyes and
a heavy beard" and he had "a large scar below the left eye."

Over the next four decades this Franciscan, Padre Narciso
Duran, would emerge as the last great leader of the mission
chain. He built San Jose into one of the largest, most successful missions in Alta California, served three times as Father
President of all the missions and played a central role keeping the mission network functioning after secularization.

This capable man also became known as "the padre musi-
cian par excellence," even though he had no professional
training in music. Early in his tenure at San Jose, Duran created a system that enabled the Indians to learn to sing European music. He would spend a couple hours, several days of
the week, training young neophytes to sing. He composed the
first choir book in California. The San Jose Mission Choir
became famous under his leadership. The group consisted of
young Indian boys, accompanied by 30 Indians playing vio-
lins, flutes, trumpets and drums.

Duran was born in Castellon de Ampurias in Catalonia,
Spain on Dec. 16, 1776. He was ordained in Barcelona in 1800,
and volunteered for the American missions shortly there-

after. He set sail for Vera Cruz Mexico in May 1803. He completed the customary missionary training at San Fernando College in Mexico City and arrived at the port of Monterey in June 1806.

THE MISSION OF ST. JOSE was founded in 1797 and had in 1829, a population of about 2,000 Indians. It possesses some of the best lands in the country for agricultural purposes, from which is obtained an immense quantity of grain. It frequently supplies the Russian company, who yearly sends three or four large ships for stores for their northern settlements. In the rear of the establishment is a large reservoir of excellent water, which is carried, through pipes, to the gardens and other parts of the mission. In front of the church is a very neat fountain, and also conveniences for washing and bathing. In point of beauty, the buildings here were very inferior to those of the southern missions. Durability and convenience alone seem to have been consulted in their construction, and they mostly presented a very ordinary appearance.

The padre, Father Narciso Duran, a venerable old man . . . had spent the most part of his life in incessant labor, to promote the advancement of his holy religion. Generous, kind and benevolent, the natives not only revered him as their spiritual father and friend, but also seemed almost to adore him. He was universally beloved . . . while many a transient traveler blessed him, and thanked God that such a man existed among them.

🦋 Alfred Robinson describing San Jose in 1829 in his book *Life in California*

Alta California was still under Spanish rule in 1806, although the level of support was declining. Under Duran's leadership San Jose became a model for how a mission could become self-sufficient. After completing a new church to give a focus to the mission, Duran embarked on a 22-year expansion of San Jose. First, the padres and neophytes dammed Mission Creek and created an elaborate irrigation system. Then they increased the amount of land under cultivation,

MIssion San Jose

and expanded the number of cattle and sheep. Soon San Jose had the third largest livestock herd in the mission chain. A flour mill, soap factory and tannery were also built at the mission. A large Indian village for the growing neophyte population was constructed, and by the time Duran left San Jose, the neophyte population had grown to more than 1,800 (the second largest in the mission chain.)

143

Despite his accomplishments, Duran became embroiled in a conflict with the neophytes in the 1820s. Once Spanish support stopped after the Mexican takeover in 1821, agricultural and livestock production was increased so the mission could trade hides and tallow for other necessities. The added production required more neophytes to do the work. Unfortunately "European diseases" were decimating the population, and frightening the surviving Indians, many of whom tried to escape. The missions struggled to prevent the exodus. There were increasingly vigorous efforts to return runaways and capture "pagan" Indians. Treatment of the Indians by unpaid soldiers became increasingly harsh.

The largest revolt of neophytes to confront Duran was in 1828. Estanislao, a neophyte who was one of the Indian alcade (essentially a policeman) of Mission San Jose, organized an uprising that year. No less than 500 Indians from San Jose, Santa Cruz and San Juan Bautista left their missions and joined some non-mission Indians in the San Joaquin Valley. Their plan was to free all Indians. It took three military expeditions to quell the revolt, which finally was ended in 1829.

Duran was caught off guard by the revolt. He had developed close relationships with many of the neophytes and had a reputation for being fair. When Estanislao was finally captured Duran intervened to seek a pardon for him. Estanislao returned to the mission and is said to have lived there until his death in 1850.

San Jose continued to be viable mission during the Mexican period. Richard Henry Dana discussed the mission's success in hide trading in *Two Years before the Mast*. Because of the fame of Duran's choir, and the proximity of San Jose to the Monterey headquarters of Alta California, many foreign visitors came to San Jose.

As his reputation grew, Duran was asked to take on special assignments. In 1812, he investigated the murder of Padre Andre Quintana at Mission Santa Cruz. Duran also accompanied the 1817 expedition that explored the Sacramento and San Joaquin rivers, searching for new mission sites and was present when San Rafael was established that year. In 1823, he helped stop a plot to close Mission Dolores and Mission San Rafael in favor of a new mission at Sonoma.

Duran was chosen to be the new President of the California missions in 1825. Initially he ran the missions from San Jose, but in 1833, he had relocate to Mission Santa Barbara. The Mexican government had transferred control of all the missions north of San Miguel to Mexican Franciscans

Duran served at Mission Santa Barbara in various capacities over the rest of his life. He served as Mission President (three times,) was appointed principal liaison with territorial government (with title of Commissary Prefect) and (in 1845) Vicar General of the newly formed diocese of California.

IN THE MISSION BUILDING, which is now in ruin, we found, reduced to a state of greatest want, the oldest Spanish Franciscan of California, the Rev. Father Ramon Abella. The mission has suffered such devastations that the poor friar was bedded on an ox-hide, and used the horn of an ox as a drinking cup, and for nourishment had only some strips of meat dried in the sun. The venerable father distributes the little that is sent to him among some Indian children, who with their parents, occupy the tumble-down houses that surround the mission. Several kind-hearted persons and the Rev. Father Presidente Duran himself have offered a home and comfort to Father Abella, but he always declines and says that he wants to die at his post.

🦋 Eugene Duflot de Mofras, who visited San Luis Obispo in 1841

Duran became a prominent figure in Santa Barbara in his final years. One contemporary, Augustias de la Guerra y Ord, wrote, "Father Duran made everyone love him to the point that all were willing to sacrifice for him . . . .. He accomplished many things during his long life, particularly after the political upheaval, especially the winning of minds and prevention of flowing of blood. He could not always quiet the tempest, but I can only believe that his good advice and influence contributed to making these disturbances less deplorable."

Duran tried to avoid secularization of the missions, but the Mexicans finally removed Franciscan control in 1834, and in subsequent years the mission system steadily dissolved. The extensive land holdings were dispersed, with many land grants going to Mexican officials. Under Governor Pio Pico, the mission's buildings were rented to civilians and ultimately sold. Between 1834 and 1845 Duran worked to keep the mission churches open and staffed. He also became a vigorous advocate of the rights of the Indians.

Duran lived through every phase of the mission era, and was a central player in most of the key events. He saw the completion of the Alta California mission chain, and was the only Father President to preside over all 21 missions. The missions became self-sufficient under his leadership, but that very success made the ultimate takeover of the mission lands inevitable. He steered the missions through the turbulent years of Mexican control and secularization of the missions, and lived to see the complete destruction of the system.

Fr. Narciso Duran died at on June 1, 1846 at the age of 70. A few months later the American flag was raised in Monterey, and his beloved missions would begin a long, slow process of return, restoration and rebirth.

REFERENCES:

Franciscan Missionaries in Hispanic California by Maynard Geiger, O.F.M, San Marino: Huntington Library, 1969.

Expedition on the Sacramento and San Joaquin Rivers in 1817 by Narciso Duran, translated by C.E. Chapman, Berkeley, 1911.

Life in California by Alfred Robinson, San Francisco, 1891.

AS IN ALL OTHER DEPARTMENTS OF LIFE, there were shadows in the relatively small group of this corps of 142 missionaries. By far the greater number persevered with fidelity to their vows of priesthood and Franciscan life. At the top we find the leaders, men of talent, ability and eminent virtue, who accomplished great things against overwhelming odds, six of whom sacrificed their lives, while most were in a dangerously exposed condition. The preponderance might be classed as men of ordinary ability, zeal, learning and virtue. They were good and faithful workers. Only one Spaniard, toward the close of the mission period, bears the proven stigma of immorality; two became alcoholics, one of whom attempted suicide. Two became miscreant in behavior, who evidently needed psychiatric treatment as well as paternal correction. The range of character and personal characteristics was wide and diversified.

The Zacatecans (Mexican Franciscans who took over administration of the missions from Soledad to Sonoma starting in 1833, after secularization) as a class, were inferior. Four of the 11 had reputations for immorality and other unclerical behavior. Three others have reputations for great probity, even saintliness.

🦋 Father Maynard Geiger, O.F.M., *Franciscan Missionaries in Hispanic California*, 1969

San Juan Capistrano

Jose Antonio Aguirre provided financial support to the missions during the years when California was a province of Mexico, and government supports for the missions ceased.

CHAPTER 19

DON ANTONIO AGUIRRE

A successful importer who supported the
missions and the Catholic church in its
darkest days

By 1840 the Spanish missions in Alta California were in serious trouble, after almost 20 years of Mexican rule. Mexican Franciscans and a few of the Spanish priests who swore loyalty to the Mexican Franciscans were still ministering to a dwindling flock of neophytes. Padre Narciso Duran, the last Father President of the chain, fought to keep the remaining missions open.

Duran was making an official visit to Mission San Diego in January 1840 when he became seriously ill. Fortunately for Duran, a tall, fair-skinned aristocratic gentleman, was traveling in the area with his servant, and happened to stop at the mission. Recognizing Duran's poor health, the gentleman loaded the padre into his carriage, and brought him to the San Diego Presidio where he could be nursed back to health.

Over the next 20 years this gentleman, Don Antonio Aguirre, would come to the aid of other padres in the waning days of the California missions. Surviving records show that he twice saved Mission San Juan Capistrano by providing supplies from one of his ships, and loaning money to the resident padre, Jose Maria Zalvidea, to buy food. He also helped Padre Tomas Estenaga buy clothes for the neophytes left at Mission San Gabriel. Aguirre also supported the first Catholic bishop in Alta California, Garcia Diego, serving as treasurer of the building fund. When church funds were confiscated by Mexico, Aguirre lent the Catholic church $26,000 to support the missionary fathers in Alta California.

Don Antonio bought land close to New Town Road in San Diego in 1858 and personally paid for the construction of an adobe church. By this time the Mission San Diego church was in sorry shape and not used regularly for services.

Who was this friend of the missions and wealthy aristocrat, Jose Antonio Aguirre?

Don Antonio Aguirre

Aguirre was born in San Sebastian de Viscaya, in Spain, in 1799. He moved to Louisiana at the age of 15, and then relocated to Mexico where he became a successful importer. When Mexico finally won its independence from Spain, Aguirre was expelled, and he lost all of his land. He returned to New Orleans and became an American citizen on Jan. 29, 1831. He planned to start a new business in the Mexican providence of Alta California, taking hides and tallow in trade for goods he would import from China and Peru.

Aguirre bought a ship in 1833, which he called the Leonidas. In 1834, he sailed into San Diego Bay with a load of goods, and set up his business. He quickly became close friends with the prominent families in San Diego, which was still a small provincial town of some 40 families. His business flourished and he soon built a warehouse and acquired other ships. Still unmarried, he met Maria Francisca Estudillo. The bride's father was Administrator of Mission San Luis Rey, and it is believed they were married at that mission, then settled

AGUIRRE BRINGS BISHOP TO SANTA BARBARA

The schooner Leonidas arrived from St. Diego. Her owner, Don Jose Antonio Aguirre, had lately been married there and was bringing his wife to Santa Barbara, where he had been preparing a suitable residence. The venerable Bishop (Francisco Garcia Diego) and his retinue had been invited to accompany the bridal party . . . and all were anxious for the Bishop's arrival, for he was a functionary that but very few in California had ever beheld.

The vessel was in sight on the morning of the 11th of January 1842. All was bustle; men, women, and children hastened to the beach, banners flying, drums beating and soldiers marching. The whole population of the place turned out to pay homage to this first Bishop of California. At 11 o'clock the vessel anchored, the Bishop came on shore and was welcomed by the kneeling multitude. All received his benediction – all kissed the pontifical ring. The troops, and civilian authorities then escorted him to the home of Don Jose Antonio, where he dined. The females had formed, with ornamented canes, beautiful arches, through which the procession passed.

The bride, with her mother and her sisters, remained on board (the Leonidas)all afternoon, when they, also, repaired to the festive scene.

At 4 o'clock the Bishop was escorted to the Mission . . . when, a short distance from the town, the enthusiastic inhabitants took the horses from his carriage, and dragged it themselves.

❧ Alfred Robinson, *Life in California*

in Santa Barbara where he built his bride a magnificent house, La Casa de Aguirre.

Tragedy struck in October 1842 when his wife died in childbirth. Father Duran, who was still administering the mission chain from Mission Santa Barbara, performed last rites. Donna Francisca was the first woman to be interred in the crypt of the Mission Santa Barbara chapel.

Aguirre threw himself back into business, and never returned to the house he had built for his beloved bride. Aguirre's good fortune finally returned in 1843 when he received his first rancho grant (48,800 acres.) He hired a ranch foreman for the property and began to acquire more land. By the time of the American takeover of California in 1846, Aguirre owned more than 150,000 acres of land.

That same year, Aguirre remarried. His new wife, Rosario Estudillo, was the younger sister of his first wife. The couple settled in San Diego and their first baby was born in 1849. The couple would eventually have seven children. As his family grew, Aguirre retired from the sea and concentrated on other ventures. He and several partners developed San Diego's New Town. He also is credited with building the first wharf in San Diego.

Aguirre's health began to fail in 1860. He made out his will naming Donna Rosario, his loyal wife, guardian of his children and executrix of his estate. He died July 31, 1860 and was buried in the adobe church at Mission San Diego. His wife moved to one of the ranchos where she spent the rest of her life.

Aguirre represents the best of the major landholders who emerged in the decades following secularization of the missions. He was a self-made man, and an astute businessman, generous to the poor and supportive of the Catholic Church. The missions in Southern California benefited from his generosity and support in their darkest years.

REFERENCES:

"Don Jose Antonio Aguirre: Spanish Merchant and Ranchero" by Mary H. Haggland in the *Journal of San Diego History*, Volume 29, #1. This is available online at http://www.sandiegohistory.org/bio/aguirrejournal.htm

History of California (7 vols.) by Hubert Howe Bancroft, San Francisco: The History Co., Publishers, 1886; facsimile printing, Santa Barbara, 1963.

Pico House in Downtown Los Angeles
The first hotel in Los Angeles was built by former governor Pio Pico.

CHAPTER 20

PIO PICO

The last, and most corrupt governor of California during the Mexican era, who was still selling mission buildings days before the Americans occupied Monterey in July 1846

After Mexico won its independence from Spain in 1821, the revolutionary government attempted to control Alta California by sending politicians from Mexico to rule the territory. The holdover Spanish governor, Pablo Vicente Sola, was replaced on Nov. 22, 1822. Over the next 24 years a succession of political appointees and self-serving administrators – 15 governors in all – enriched themselves at the expense of the Indians.

The worst of the sorry lot was Pio Pico, the last governor of Mexican California. Pico scrambled to sell mission buildings right up until a few days before the American occupation of California began in July 1846.

The years following the Mexican takeover of the missions were confusing times. Governors followed one another in rapid succession. The lines of authority were unclear. There was constant tension between the north (Monterey, the historic headquarters; the growing city of San Francisco; and Sonoma, the base of General Mariano Vallejo) and the south. Small-scale revolutions erupted as men jockeyed for power and the "Californios" (the generation born in California) pushed for greater self-rule. Adding to the confusion, a strong anti-clerical element in Mexico constantly lobbied for the secularization of the missions.

Secularization had worked in other parts of the Spanish Empire. On the surface, secularization was an orderly process. The mission church and padre's quarters were turned over to local clergy, to be operated as a parish. An administrator would then manage the other buildings in the complex for the benefit of the public. Land was set aside at each former mission for a town, with ample acreage for community grazing lands and agriculture. Indian neophytes were to receive the rest of the land, with plots allocated to each family. In California, secularization was a disaster.

Secularization was delayed in the early years of Mexican rule because the missions were the primary source of food and the only economically viable institutions in the territory. The padres also argued forcefully that the Indians were not ready to function as independent property owners. So, even as late as 1830, the mission system was largely intact. In fact, throughout Alta California there were only 21 pieces of property in private hands.

When secularization was finally ordered in 1833, it was implemented unevenly and unfairly. Most of the Indians were quickly swindled out of their lands, which came into the hands of speculators. The relatives and friends of each reigning governor were the beneficiaries of large land grants. The wealthy, and the politically connected, were able to assemble large holdings. Mission Indians became employed at the ranches of Californios like Pico, or they simply escaped to the interior.

Pico figured prominently in the history of the period. He was born in 1801 at Mission San Gabriel, the fourth of 10 children. He was the son of a soldier, Jose Maria Pico, who came from Mexico with the Anza expedition. Like many of the offspring of common soldiers recruited in Mexico, he was of mixed blood – part Native American, part African and part Hispanic.

EXAMPLES OF GOV. PICO'S SALE OF MISSION PROPERTIES

Pio Pico illegally sold Mission Santa Ines to Jose M. Covarrubias and Jose Joaquin Carillo in June 1846 for the paltry sum of $7,000. This took place three weeks before the United States troops entered California; the sale was later declared invalid.

Andres Pico, brother of the governor, and Juan Manso, took a nine-year lease on San Fernando Rey in December 1845 . . . for an annual stipend of $1,120 . . . and "bought" the property in 1856. Pico and his family utilized the mission convent building as one their summer residences. In 1853 the Bishop of Monterey instituted a lawsuit to recover the mission buildings for the church . . . but the complicated and drawn out legal preceding was not settled until May 31, 1862 (when) President Abraham Lincoln . . . restored the requested properties to the church.

Pico disposed of the San Juan Capistrano property in December 1845 by selling it to his brother-in-law, John Foster, for $710. Foster lived in the mission for 20 years in what is presently the gift shop. The church was allowed to keep the Serra Church and a small room as a residence for the priest. The mission was restored to the church in 1864.

Pico sold the San Luis Obispo buildings in 1845 for $510 . . . the mission was returned to the church by the U.S. Land Commission in 1859.

Pico sold what was left of the San Luis Rey complex in 1846 for $2,437, although true inventoried value was estimated at more than $200,000.

    ❦ Information collected by Donald Francis Toomey and summarized in his book *The Spell of California's Spanish Colonial Missions.*

Pico grew to manhood in the waning days of Spanish rule. His generation welcomed the Mexican revolt against Spain, and benefited from the turmoil that would follow. Pico first came to prominence in 1832 when he was elected "interim" governor (he served only 20 days) during one of the first local revolts. Over the next 10 years, using his connections and power, he amassed large land holdings and became a prominent rancher in the San Fernando Valley. Pico managed to get himself appointed Mission Administrator of San Luis Rey, where he plundered the mission property.

Pico became governor in 1845 following yet another revolt by the Californios that forced out the last Mexican-appointed governor, Manuel Micheltorena. The revolt ended in an artillery duel at Cahuenga Pass, near the present-day location of Universal Studios.

When Pico took office, secularization had been essentially completed, but the new governor found additional ways to profit from what was left of the missions. He engineered the sale of former mission buildings held in trust by the government, often at bargain basement prices, and ended up owning many mission buildings.

Governor Pico tried unsuccessfully to slow migration into California. He spoke publicly against newcomers. "What are we to do then? Shall we remain supine, while these daring strangers are overrunning our fertile plains and gradually outnumbering and displacing us? Shall these incursions go on un-checked until we shall become strangers in our own land," he said. In the tumultuous final year of the Mexican period, Pico maneuvered to get California taken over by France or Britain . . . since the European powers would be more likely to keep California an agrarian society, managed by large land-holders (like himself). Pico, in one of his last speeches, criticized American immigrants who "are cultivating farms, establishing vineyards, erecting mills, sawing up lumber, building workshops and doing a thousand other things, which seem natural to them, but which Californians neglect or despise."

When the American Pacific Fleet occupied Monterey, Pico organized resistance in the south. After the Americans occupied Los Angeles, which he had made the state capital, Pico escaped to Mexico.

In his final term in office, Pico stepped up his assault on the missions. Mission buildings became storage sheds, personal residences, stagecoach stops, business offices, even taverns and dancehalls.

Pio Pico

Events at Mission San Miguel had particularly tragic consequences. Three days before the U.S. flag was raised in Monterey, Pico sold all of Mission San Miguel, except the church and padre's quarters. One of the buyers was an Englishman, William Reed, a cattle and sheep rancher. Reed and his family lived in a wing of the mission through 1848, occasionally renting rooms to men traveling to the gold fields. In December 1848, a party of five men stayed at the mission for five nights. The men overheard Reed bragging about his wealth. The five men left to continue on their journey, but that evening they doubled back to Mission San Miguel under cover of darkness, murdering Reed, his entire family and six servants as they searched for money and gold. A posse caught up with the gang, who had fled south. Two of the men were killed in the ensuing fight, and the other three taken to Santa Barbara where they were hung.

Pico had quietly moved back to California to protect his interests in late 1848. As a private citizen he became a businessman, and for a time, served on the Los Angeles City Council.

However his dissolute ways finally caught up with him. Gambling losses forced him to sell his major holding, a ranch

159

in the San Fernando Valley. Records confirm that Pico deeded his last mission property, buildings at San Gabriel, to two Americans to pay a debt.

Pico's last big gamble was the development of the first deluxe hotel in downtown Los Angeles, what became known as Pico House. He eventually lost the hotel and his home, El Ranchito, located in present-day Whittier.

Pio Pico died in poverty in 1894, at age 93. In what many consider a fitting end, he was buried in a pauper's grave.

REFERENCES:

The Spell of California's Spanish Colonial Missions by Don Toomey. Details Pico's sale of mission buildings.

A History of California: The Spanish Period by Charles Chapman, New York: Macmillian & Co., 1921. One of the early comprehensive histories of California.

The Secularization of the California Missions by Gerald Joseph Geary. Washington, D.C.: Catholic University of America, 1934. Comprehensive, scholarly work.

THE AMERICANS

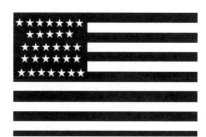

1848-Present

Mexico ceded California to the United States in February 1848, in the Treaty of Guadalupe Hidalgo. American troops had occupied California since mid 1846, camping at several of the old missions.

In January 1848 gold was discovered in California, and by 1849, 80,000 prospectors had rushed to the area, transforming the small port of San Francisco into the first major city on the West Coast. California became a state in1850.

The missions were largely ignored as settlers poured into California and America realized its "manifest destiny." A fraction of the original mission lands—the church and some surrounding acres—was returned to the Catholic Church in presidential decrees and land commission rulings between 1859-62. As a practical matter little changed with the return of the mission property. Most of the missions were already abandoned or functioning as parish churches. In time several missions were "modernized" with ungainly steeples, and a couple torn down entirely to make way for new parish churches. Interest in the missions revived toward the end of the 19th century, but it would take 50 years of sustained effort to restore these historic structures. Today the missions stand intact, as treasured icons of a proud historic past and major tourist destinations.

The central characters in the early years of American rule were men from the Mexican era who supported the transition, and American military leaders. The dominant players, who saved the missions for posterity, emerged toward the end of 19th century: Indian activists who took up the cause of the mission Indians; artists, novelists and playwrights who romanticized the Spanish era; gifted painters and early photographers who created compelling images of the crumbling structures; civic leaders who provided the funds for mission restoration and the master restorer who led the restoration effort.

The U.S. soldier whom provided behind the scenes support for the 1846 Bear Flag Revolution and who played a decisive role in the subsequent military campaign to occupy California was **John Charles Fremont**. Fremont continued to play a central role in the early history of California, serving as one of two senators when California became a state in 1850.

The story of the missions over the next 40 years is a sad tale. The missions buildings continued to suffer from decay and neglect. While a few structures remained intact, many more become abandoned ruins. The neophytes continued to drift away through the 1840s as the padres died out. A few locations survived as monasteries and seminaries, but others were put to less noble uses.

The nation was preoccupied with the realization of its manifest destiny, the industrial revolution and then the U.S. Civil War and its aftermath, during the decades after it acquired California. As the end of century approached, however, interest in the Spanish era revived. Several Indian activists like journalist **Charles Fletcher Lummis** and writer **Helen Hunt Jackson** led the crusade. Jackson published a romantic novel *Ramona* in 1884. The mission ruins were the backdrop for a love story that gripped America and made the public aware of the plight of these historic structures.

A number of talented painters – **Henry Chapman Ford**, **Chris Jorgensen** and **Edward Deakin** in particular—produced poignant depictions of the missions in their ruined states. Early photographers like **Carleton E. Watkins** and **Adam Clark Vroman** used the new medium to show what was left of the missions to a larger audience. Groups were formed to "save" the missions by men like Lummis, who organized the Landmark Club for that purpose. Not to be outdone, the women of California, under the inspired leadership of **Mrs. A.S.C. Forbes** decided to mark and preserve the historic road that connected the missions, El Camino Real. The missions were kept in the forefront of public consciousness by outdoor plays such as an annual Ramona pageant in Helmut. *The Mission Play*, written by poet **John Steven McGroarty**, was the biggest extravaganza. First staged in 1912, *The Mission Play* told the story of the missions in a three-hour musical. It ran for 20 years at a special playhouse built near the old Mission San Gabriel.

163

The actual restoration of each mission is an individual story with its own false starts and partial restorations extending over several decades. Behind the scenes wealthy benefactors like newspaper magnate **William Randolph Hearst** donated land and money to the missions. Major artists created statues of key figures from the Spanish era. The sculptor **Jo Mora** created a sarcophagus for Mission Carmel in 1922. It shows a recumbent Junipero Serra on his deathbed, surrounded by three fellow missionaries. The 1932 appointment of the talented master restorer, **Harry Downie**, as curator of Mission Carmel was a seminal event. Downie not only restored Mission Carmel between 1932-57, he guided the restoration of San Luis Obispo, San Juan Bautista and San Buenaventura—all three defaced by modernization. He helped rebuilt Mission Soledad between 1954-63 and provided the primary expertise for the extensive restoration of

San Antonio de Padua, which began in 1948 with a sizeable grant from the Hearst Foundation.

Today all the missions—in two instances replicas but for the most part fully restored original churches, padre's quarters and in a few blessed instances full mission complexes—are available to enable a new generation to visit and appreciate California's past.

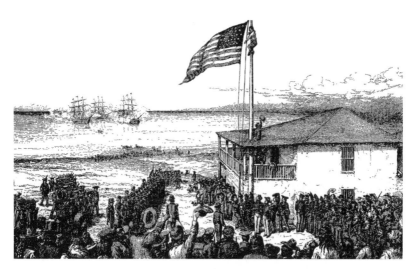

Alexander Harmer's 19th century drawing of the raising of the U.S. Flag in Monterey on July 7, 1846. Source: Missions and Missionaries of California by Fr. Zephrin Engelhardt

165

Bear Flag Monument

In June, 1846, a band of settlers revolted against Mexican rule and raised a Bear Flag on the square of Sonoma, across from Mission Solano. John Fremont provided behind-the-scenes support for the rebellion.

CHAPTER 21

JOHN CHARLES FREMONT

The American army officer-pathfinder who
charted trails to the west and played a decisive
role in the American takeover of California

O n a bitter, overcast day in early March 1843, a half-starved band of 39 American soldiers and survey-ors arrived at Sutter's Fort on the Sacramento River. John Charles Fremont, a 32-year-old lieutenant, was in charge of the party. Ignoring advice from his Indian guides, he had led his men across the Rockies in the dead of winter, eager to carry out his orders: To survey the largely unknown region between the Rocky Mountains and the Pacific Ocean. The Americans rested and re-provisioned over the next sev-eral weeks, then crossed the Sierra Nevada range to return to their base in Kansas, arriving in July 1844.

Fremont would play a pivotal role in the future of California.

The situation in California in 1843 was highly unstable. The Mexican government—caught up in its own revolution—appointed one incompetent governor after another to admin-ister the territory. The reigning governor, Manuel Micheltorena, was very unpopular with the "Californios" who had the real power. The mission lands were largely in private hands, and the next governor, Pio Pico, the most corrupt of a sorry lot, would sell off many of the remaining mission build-ings to line his pockets.

At the time, the major maritime powers including Great Britain, France and the United States were each maneuvering to take over California.

Immigrants from the United States had begun to filter into northern California in increasing numbers with the quiet encouragement of General Mariano Vallejo, who saw that a union with the United States was inevitable. Almost 2,000 of the 2,500 "foreigners" in California were American.

Upon his return to Washington, Fremont was given the double rank of first lieutenant and captain and asked to organize another expedition to explore the California territory more thoroughly. That spring, he headed west again. After another arduous journey he arrived in California in the winter of 1845. This time he left his men in the San Joaquin Valley and rode to Monterey to obtain permission from the Mexican authorities to survey. Permission was granted then almost immediately revoked.

The Mexicans were nervous about having an armed party of Americans wandering around their thinly soldiered territory. Fremont was ordered to leave the country without delay. The order was refused, and the Mexicans assembled a force under Col. Jose Castro to drive out the Americans. Fremont hastily built a rude fort of trees on Hawk's Peak, 30 miles from Monterey. After a lot of rhetoric, Fremont withdrew "slowly and growlingly" and made his way through the Sacramento Valley to Oregon.

On May 9, 1846, a dispatch rider caught up with Fremont and delivered explicit instructions that he was to watch over U.S. interests in California. Washington had learned of a plot to transfer California to Great Britain. There were also rumors that Castro intended to destroy the American settlements on the Sacramento River.

Fremont immediately returned to California where he learned that Castro was indeed marching toward Sacramento.

Fremont, who by now had been promoted to lieutenant colonel, set up camp, blocked Castro and quietly encouraged the settlers to take charge of their own destiny.

John Charles Fremont

In anticipation of the ultimate U.S. takeover, a group of 30 trappers and local settlers (mostly Americans) occupied the town of Sonoma and arrested General Mariano Vallejo. The settler's declared California a republic on June 14 and raised a flag containing a crude drawing of a bear. A group of 50 Californios sent by Castro skirmished with the settlers in what became known as the Battle of Olompali. Fremont openly supported the "Bear Flaggers."

169

Fremont crossed San Francisco Bay (coining the phrase the Golden Gate) and occupied the Presidio in San Francisco.

What no one realized was that the United States was already at war with Mexico. Hostilities began with a dispute over the United States' annexation of Texas. In January 1846, Mexican troops attacked the forces of Zachary Taylor who had occupied disputed territory near the Rio Grande River. On May 13, 1846, Congress declared war on Mexico. The war was to last two years.

General Winfield Scott and his army fought the decisive battles of the war, as they marched from Veracruz to Puebla, finally capturing Mexico City itself in August 1847. The hostilities accelerated the takeover of California.

Word of the war with Mexico reached the U.S. Pacific Fleet in June. By July 2, Commodore John Sloat was at Monterey and on July 7, he declared that henceforth California would be part of the United States. The California Republic had lasted less than a month.

Fremont learned of Sloat's occupation of Monterey on July 10 and hurried there with 160 mounted riflemen. Fremont was asked to organize a California battalion and he was also made civil governor of the territory.

Castro and Pico fled to Mexico and it looked for a while like the takeover of California would be bloodless. Unfortunately, the American rule was heavy handed, and the Californios in Southern California mounted a resistance that lasted for four months, winning two decisive battles. The Californios finally surrendered to Fremont in the San Fernando Valley on July 13, 1856. Fremont signed the formal articles of capitulation on Jan. 13, 1847. During much of the period, Fremont's troops were quartered in the old Mission San Fernando Rey.

The United States war with Mexico formally ended Feb. 2, 1848 with the signing of the treaty of Guadalupe Hidalgo. Mexico ceded 58 percent of its entire territory (present day Arizona, California, New Mexico, Texas and parts of Colorado, Nevada and Utah) in exchange for $15 million.

Meanwhile, Fremont became entangled in a dispute between the naval commander, Commodore Robert Field Stockton, who succeeded Sloat, and General Stephen Watts Kearney, his superior in the regular army. Fremont was ultimately court-martialed and forced to resign his commission in October 1848.

Fremont was not done with California, however. In 1848, Fremont organized another expedition across the continent, at his expense, to find a practical passage to California. He reached Sacramento in the spring of 1849, determined to settle there. Fremont was elected to the U.S. Senate from California and took his seat on Sept. 10, 1850, the day after California was admitted as a state.

By this point in his life, Fremont had become one of the most famous and popular explorers in U.S. history.

His beginnings were humble. He grew up as the illegitimate child of a prominent Virginia society woman, Anne Beverly Whiting, and a penniless French refugee. He was born in Savannah Georgia January 21,1813.

Fremont strove for respectability all his life. He was a social climber and skillful self-promoter. After completing college, he joined the U.S. Topographical Corps, participating in a military reconnaissance of Cherokee country in Georgia, North Carolina and Tennessee. He was commissioned on July 7, 1838. In 1840, while in Washington, he met and became engaged to Jessie Benton, daughter of Thomas H. Benton, the senior senator from Missouri, who ultimately became his most important sponsor. Fremont was then given a series of assignments to explore the West, and published reports on his trips to a public eager to see the United States expand westward. He became known as the Pathfinder. He married Jessie in 1841.

After his brief term as a U.S. Senator, Fremont traveled extensively in Europe where he was honored for his discoveries. He led another expedition to California in 1853, opening up additional routes to that state. Fremont and his family took up residency in New York in 1855, in an effort to further his political ambitions. He became a candidate for president of the United States, winning the popular vote, but losing the election to James Buchanan who garnered more electoral votes.

Shortly after the beginning of the Civil War, Fremont was called back into the army as a major general. During the war, he served in Missouri, fought Stonewall Jackson in the battle of Cross Keys and was appointed, but declined, a key position in the Army of Virginia.

Fremont remained a visible public figure for the rest of his life. His autobiography *Memoirs of My Life,* published in 1886, was a best seller. Fremont died in 1890.

I ARRIVED AT THE MISSION SAN LUIS REY in the afternoon, being built on a tableland overlooking an extensive valley. The mission buildings have a very imposing appearance and are built in the ancient Spanish style. The interior of the mission is in very good condition. Near the buildings are a few huts in which live some Indian families. Having been informed I might find entertainment at the house of an American, named Tibbets, about one-half mile from here, I rode down and finding this to be the case, I dismounted. This man is married to a native woman and raises a quantity of water and muskmelons that were just ripe. Not having any accommodations in his house for strangers, I mounted the haystack in which I slept like a prince.

In the morning I went up to the mission with the intention of taking a sketch and where I found stationed a sergeant and two soldiers – all Irishmen in Uncle Sam's service, who were sent here to guard the mission buildings and what remains in it against robbers and vandalism.

On the 14th of September I left San Luis Rey for San Diego. At 8 o'clock in the evening I arrived at San Diego, where I dismounted at the public house of a Mr. Rose, a German and a man of considerable enterprise, who dabbles in everything. He owns a number of houses, has purchased several thousands of town lots at the most desirable spot at the entrance to the harbor from the sea, with the expectation of making millions if the eastern railroad might terminate here. He has several ranchos, a tannery, and a public house, is boring for bituminous coal and an artesian well, sends out hunters, etc., and seems to be a clever kind of man who keeps this otherwise dull little town somewhat alive. The town has about 2,500 inhabitants, who seem to get poorer every day. At some future time San Diego cannot fail to become a place of great importance.

I took a sketch of the town, after which I went to the mission, which lies in an easterly direction from here, about 6 miles distance, on the end of a fine valley full of pasture. The mission buildings have lost their ancient appearance, having been renovated by the government, and serve now as the quarters of U.S. troops.

❦ Account of a Tour of the California Missions and Towns – 1856 – *The Journal & Drawings of Henry Miller*

REFERENCES:

John Charles Fremont by Olive Burt, New York, NY: Jullian Messner, 1955. A thorough and balanced account of Fremont's life.

Pathfinder by Tom Chaffin, Hill & Wang, 2002. This new biography is a great read. Chaffin's account of Fremont's expeditions are gripping; his story of Fremont's relationship with his wife Jessie reveals a genuine love story.

The 11-page on-line biography of Fremont in the Virtual War Museum, edited by A.C. Image is comprehensive. See http://www.johnfremont.com

San Antonio de Padua – 1895

The decay and ruin of magnificent missions like San Antonio de Padua inspired Charles Lummis to raise money for mission restoration.

CHAPTER 22

CHARLES FLETCHER LUMMIS

Newspaperman and promoter of California
who founded the Landmarks Club in 1895,
dedicated to restoring the missions and other
historic California structures

A 25-year-old reporter at the Cincinnati, Ohio *Scioto Gazette*, the "oldest newspaper west of the Allegheny Mountains," was pondering his future in the summer of 1884. He wanted to move to California, but didn't have the money to travel there. He wanted to write for a more "prominent" paper, but didn't have any contacts.

Charles Fletcher Lummis was never without an idea, however, and he had plenty of chutzpah. He wrote Col. Harrison Gray Otis, the publisher of what was then called *The Los Angeles Daily Times*. Otis was a former Ohioan, and Lummis used that tenuous connection between them to introduce himself. He started sending copies of his articles to Otis. He wrote a series of letters summarizing his qualifications. To ingratiate himself with Otis, a prominent member of the Republican Party, he underscored his role as president of the local Young Men's Republican Club. But, what finally hooked Otis was a bold proposal. Showing the genius for self-promotion he would display all his life, Lummis revealed that he planned to walk the 3,507 miles to Los Angeles, to see the country, get in shape and generate material for future stories.

Otis liked the young man's ambition and told him he would hire him as a reporter if he made it to Los Angeles. *The Scioto Gazette*, however, hated the plan and fired Lummis before he could resign. Lummis then cut a deal with that paper's rival, the *Chillicothe Leader.* The Leader agreed to publish weekly dispatches from Lummis as he "tramped" across the country, paying $5 for each story.

To call attention to himself and his bold journey, Lummis decided to wear a distinctive outfit. It consisted of knicker-bockers and red knee-high stockings and a white flannel shirt tied at the neck with a blue ribbon. He purchased a wide brimmed felt hat and a large canvas duck coat to complete the ensemble. He shipped a Winchester rifle ahead to Kansas, to carry when he began to reach "injun" country. Amazingly he decided to wear his favorite pair of low-cut dress shoes because they fit well and would toughen his feet. (the shoes didn't last.)

Lummis departed Cincinnati on Sept. 12, 1884 beginning a remarkable career as newspaperman, poet, author of 16 books, archaeologist, Indian rights advocate, champion of California's Spanish heritage and preserver of the old Spanish missions.

His trip was a grand success. He filed dispatches every week with the *Chillicothe Leader,* earning enough money to cover his expenses. He also sent periodic reports to Otis and had several articles published in the *Los Angeles Daily Times,* broadening his reputation. By the time he arrived in Los Angeles, it was clear to Otis that his new reporter was a col-orful figure who could spin a good yarn.

Lummis fell in love with the west on this trip. He admired the landscape and he was fascinated by the multi-racial cul-ture. His travel transformed his perception of the country. His friend, Harry Carr, in an obituary he wrote for the *Los Angeles Times*, pointed out that "Lummis was one of the first writers to realize that the history of the United States did not begin with Plymouth Rock, one of the first to discover the Southwest as a treasure trove of romance, history and archaeology."

Lummis also developed an enduring conviction that the area's Spanish past, particularly the early missions of the padres had to be preserved. Ten years after he arrived in Los Angeles, at the peak of his influence, Lummis set up an organization to preserve the missions and other historic structures.

Lummis had first become acquainted with the missions on his trip to Los Angeles. Over the years he had written several times of the old missions.

An opportunity to lead the charge to save the historic structures came in 1892, when Tesso Kelso, a friend, accepted a position back East. Kelso, the Los Angeles City librarian, had started to raise funds for mission restoration, but hadn't garnered much support. Lummis was asked to take custody of the funds – $90 – and immediately began to formulate big plans. He set up an organization known as the Landmarks Club. He obtained the backing of prominent California civic leaders to endorse the group, even persuading his ex- boss, Otis, to serve on the Landmarks Club Advisory Board. Lummis had joined the Times staff back in 1885 when he reached Los Angeles, and was made city editor the next year. However he grew restless at a desk job, and in 1888 became a free-lance writer. However, he and Otis remained in contact and Lummis wrote articles for the paper from time to time.

The Landmarks Club raised money from wealthy benefactors and through a membership fee ($1 a year, $25 for a life-

Charles Fletcher Lummis

time membership.) The money the club raised saved the Serra Chapel at San Juan Capistrano. The Landmarks Club bought the crumbling San Antonia de Pala asistencia in 1903, a San Luis Rey sub-mission that had fallen into private hands, and returned the unique building to the church in 1903. It is the only surviving asistencia still serving Native Americans. The Landmarks Club also funded an effort to preserve the La Purisima ruins, although a full restoration would require large-scale financing by successor organizations in the 1930s.

The Landmarks Club, under Lummis' direction, was creative in raising money. They sponsored a candle sale to raise money for the restoration of Mission San Fernando Rey, for example. No less than 6,000 people showed up on "candle day" and bought thousands of candles at $1 apiece.

Lummis promoted the cause of mission restoration in magazine articles and in public appearances. There was still an anti-Catholic sentiment in many parts of the United States

at the turn of the century, so Lummis, a lifelong protestant, positioned mission restoration as a civic effort. Lummis argued that, "These mighty piles belong not to the Catholic Church, but to you and to me, and to our children and the world. They are monuments of heroism and faith and zeal and art. Let us save them, not for the church, but for humanity." Lummis enrolled all the major Southern California religious leaders in the cause of the old missions. Ever the promoter, Lummis was successful in having both the Catholic and Episcopal bishops of Los Angeles join him on the dais at one public meeting of the Landmarks Club. When these men shook hands, it was front-page news.

Over his life Lummis championed many causes and managed to stay in the public eye. He published *A Tramp Across the Continent* in 1892; an expanded and somewhat fictionalized account of his famous trek. He became a fervent Indian rights activist. He traveled on a "scientific" expedition to Peru. Articles and books poured out of him.

He helped start a new magazine *Land of Sunshine* in 1895. The principal backer was the Los Angeles Chamber of Commerce. Lummis served as editor and major contributor. His article in the first issue was an essay entitled "The Spanish American Face." He wrote a regular column titled "In the Lion's Den," which was full of personal commentary. The early issues of the magazine were so dependent on Lummis that he used pseudonyms to create the impression there was a whole stable of staff writers. In subsequent years, Lummis attracted a stellar group of contributors and the magazine became a definite source of information on California. Over time, the scope of the magazine was expanded and it was renamed Out West in 1902.

By the end of the first decade of the new century, though, the Lummis star began to dim. His messy private life (thrice divorced) limited his job opportunities. He was eased out of the magazine he built in 1909. He popularity began to fade in the period leading up to the Spanish American War, limiting his access to an old Harvard College contact, Theodore Roosevelt. Roosevelt had been a Lummis fan and admired his position on Indian rights.

After the beginning of World War I, Lummis had to struggle to stay in the public eye, and earn enough to feed his family. What saved him was the re-issuance of some of his original books. Then through some old contacts, and his reputation as a master promoter, he was put on the advisory board of the Harvey Cars Courier Corps, set up by the Santa Fe Railroad to promote excursions in the west.

Lummis began to be bothered by a nagging sore on his cheek in 1927. It was mis-diagnosed as a spider bite. A more thorough examination concluded that Lummis had a malignant tumor. The doctors told him he had a year to live. He rushed to finish his last book *Flowers of Our Lost Romance*, a collection of essays that he had written over the course of his life.

The prolific writer died at his home on Nov. 25, 1928. Mark

Thomason reports that Lummis "left precise instructions about how his body should be handled. He wanted to be placed Indian fashion between two redwood boards that he had selected for himself, and he wanted to be wrapped in one of his favorite Indian blankets and be cremated."

At the memorial service for Lummis, the poet and future congressman, John Steven McGroarty, said that Lummis "had little faith in an afterlife, but was open to the possibility . . . as long as he didn't have to hurry there."

WHEN I FIRST STUMBLED upon the Southwest (on his 'tramp' to California, in 1884-85) it was different. The stark peaks, the bewitched valleys were as now. As now, except that the Old Life had not yet fled from them. Across those incredible acclivities, where distance loses itself and the eye is a liar, the pronghorn antelope still drifted, like a ghostly scud of great thistledown, 500 to a band. In the peaks, the cimarron still played ladder with the precipices, in the pines, the grizzly shambled shuffling, and in green rincons where valley and foothill come together, and a spring issues of their union, there were lonely adobes, with a curl of friendly smoke from their potsherd chimneys – gray, flat little homes, bald without, within warm and vocal of the Old Times when people sang because they Felt Like It.

Today the antelopes are gone, the cimarrons have yielded up their wonderful coiled horns to adorn the walls of those who didn't kill them; the grizzlies are rugs for persons who couldn't shoot a flock of barns flying low, and the songs are almost near extinction.

❧ Charles Fletcher Lummis "Catching our Archaeology Alive" in *Out West Magazine*, January 1905.

REFERENCES:

American Character: The Curious Life of Charles Fletcher Lummis and the Rediscovery of the Southwest, by Mark Thompson. Arcade Publishing, Inc. New York: 2001. This well researched entertaining new book rescues Lummis from an undeserved obscurity.

A Tramp Across the Continent by Charles Fletcher Lummis, Charles Scribner's Sons, 1892, reprinted by the University of Nebraska Press, 1982.

Charles F. Lummis: The Man and His West by Turbese Lummis and Keith Lummis, University of Oklahoma Press: Norman, OK, 1975. Reminisces by his daughter and son.

Americans and the California Dream by Kevin Starr, New York. Oxford University Press, 1973. Includes a balanced discussion of Lummis and his impact.

Santa Ines Mission

*Helen Hunt Jackson used the Spanish era and the old missions as the setting for her romantic novel **Ramona**, and argued forcefully that these storied structures needed to be saved.*

CHAPTER 23

HELEN HUNT JACKSON

Indian rights activist and author whose best selling romantic novel *Ramona* laid the groundwork for broad public support for the preservation of the old Spanish missions

Using an appointment from the president of the United States and a best-selling romantic novel she had written as platforms, Helen Hunt Jackson is credited with bringing the plight of mission Indians to the world's attention in the late 1800s.

History shows that Jackson was special, a woman ahead of her time. Noted author Antoinette May describes Jackson as "passionate, daring, defiant, an individualist who lived by her own rules, moving as freely in an age of stagecoaches and steamships as jet setters do today. Helen lived a life that few women of her day had the courage to live. In any era she would qualify as an original."

Jackson was born Helen Maria Fiske in 1830. Her family was wealthy and well educated. Her father was a Congregational minister and professor of Latin, Greek and philosophy at Amherst College. She was, by all accounts, a strong, high-spirited, self-confident young woman. She received her education at Ipswich Female Seminary in Massachusetts and Abbott Institute in New York City.

Emily Dickinson was a classmate of Jackson's at the seminary. Dickinson, who went on to became a famous poet and Jackson's best friend, would later encourage Jackson to pursue a passion for writing following the accidental death of her husband, Army Capt. Edward Bissel Hunt, in 1863. Jackson also grieved over the deaths of two young sons.

Thanks to encouragement from Dickinson, and author Thomas Wentworth Higginson, Jackson immersed herself in writing and went on to write children's stories, poems and travel sketches. She became a bit of an eccentric, often wearing a hat that contained a stuffed owl's head, and only sleeping in a bed if the head was facing north.

After living for a time in Newport, Rhode Island, Jackson moved to Colorado Springs, CO where she met the man that was to become her second husband—a wealthy banker and railroad magnet named William Sharpless Jackson.

It was after her second marriage that Jackson began what would become a life-long fascination with the American West and its Indians.

A watershed point in Jackson's life occurred in 1879 when she attended a lecture by Chief Standing Bear on the plight of the Ponca Indians. Suddenly becoming a relentless crusader on behalf of Indians, Jackson researched and published a book *A Century of Dishonor* in 1881. More of an impassioned plea for justice and an expose than balanced history, the book caused a sensation. The chapter on the Ponca's removal from their ancestral land helped stimulate a presidential commission to compensate the tribe and allow Chief Standing Bear and his followers to remain on their land. Jackson stepped up her crusade after seeing the success her book had on improving conditions for the Poncas.

Jackson received an assignment from *Century Magazine* in the fall of 1881 to do a series on California. Her travels in the state, accompanied by an illustrator, gave her a first-hand exposure to Indian life and the old missions. The plight of the mission Indians became her new cause. In 1883, President Chester Arthur appointed her a special commissioner of Indian Affairs to investigate the status of the California mission Indians. Her report was a strong indictment of federal policy, but it never garnered much public support.

Undeterred by the lack of public support for the mission Indians, Jackson became committed to "write a story that would do for the Indian what Uncle Tom's Cabin did for the Negro." She wrote to a friend about her plans for a novel that would "set forth some Indian experiences in a way to move people's hearts. People will read a novel when they will not read serious books."

Helen Hunt Jackson

And read they did. Her book *Ramona* became a best seller. The book was a moving romance story and plea for the Indian, written in an emotional tone that appealed to 19th century readers. The book also drew attention to the deplorable conditions of the old Spanish missions in Southern California. *Ramona* did not become, in the words of Jackson scholar Valerie Sherer Mathes, "the Uncle Tom's Cabin of Indian reform," but it was a huge success. The novel boosted tourism to Southern California, focused public attention on the plight of the Indians, and laid the groundwork for broad public support for the restoration of the old Spanish missions.

Shortly after the serialization of *Ramona* began in June 1884, Jackson fractured her leg and never regained her mobility. A few months after her fall, it was discovered that she had developed cancer. In her final months she wrote to her mentor Higginson, "*My Century of Dishonor* and *Ramona* are the only things I have done for which I am glad now. The rest is of no moment. They will live on and they will bear fruit. They already have."

Jackson, who turned out to be a prolific writer with 30 books and hundreds of articles to her credit, died August 12,

1885. She was buried near the summit of Mount Jackson in Colorado, a Cheyenne peak named for her.

REFERENCES:

Helen Hunt Jackson and Her Indian Reform Legacy by Valerie Sherer Mathes, University of Oklahoma Press, 1997.

Ramona by Helen Hunt Jackson. The Signet Classic Edition contains a superb forward by Michael Dorris, professor of Native American Studies at Dartmouth College, and a member of the Modoc Indian Tribe.

Helen Hunt Jackson: Writer, activist for Native Americans, an illuminating biography published online by Thomson—Gale: (http://www.galegroup.com/free-resources/whm/bio/huntjackson-h.htm).

The True Story of Ramona: Its Facts and Fictions, Inspiration and Purpose by Caryle Channing Davis and William A. Alderson. New York. Dodge Publishing Company, 1914.

THE ROAD ON WHICH they (the principal characters Ramona and her Indian lover, Alessandro) must go into old San Diego, where Father Gaspara lived, was the public road from San Diego to San Luis Rey, and they were almost sure to meet travelers on it.

But their fleet horses bore them so well, that is was not late when they reached the town. Father Gaspara's house was at the end of a long, low adobe building, which had served no mean purpose in the old presidio days, but was now fallen into decay; and all its rooms, except those occupied by the Father, had been long uninhabited. On the opposite side of the way, in a neglected weedy open, stood his chapel, a poverty stricken little place, its walls imperfectly whitewashed, decorated by a few coarse pictures and by broken sconces of looking-glass, rescued in their dilapidated condition from the mission buildings now gone utterly to ruin. In these had been put candleholders of common tin, in which a few cheap candles dimly lighted the room.

Everything about it was in unison with the atmosphere of the place, the most profoundly melancholy in all of southern California. Here was the spot where that grand old Franciscan, Padre Junipero Serra, began his work, full of the devout and ardent purpose to reclaim the wilderness and its peoples to his country and his Church; on this very beach he went up and down for those first terrible weeks, nursing the sick, praying with the dying, and burying the dead, from the pestilence-stricken Mexican ships lying in the harbor. Here he baptized his first Indian converts, and founded his first mission. The only traces now remaining of his heroic labors and hard-won successes were a pile of crumbling ruins, a few old olive-trees and palms; in less than another century even these would be gone; returned into the keeping of that mother, the earth, who puts no headstone at the most sacred of her graves.

🦋 From the novel *Ramona* by Helen Hunt Jackson, First published in 1884

San Rafael Mission—Edwin Deakin

A group of talented painters brought the plight of the missions to the attention of the general public in the late 19th century. Edwin Deakin, in particular, recreated how the missions might have looked in their prime.

CHAPTER 24

MISSION PAINTERS

Three painters of exceptional talent who
produced stunning images of the old missions
captivated the general public between 1885-1920

Around the turn of the 20th century, a remarkable body of "mission paintings" by a score of artists helped create an enduring, romantic image of Spanish California. These stunning images—etchings, watercolors, large canvas oils—were done in many styles. Most artists painted a few missions. A few produced a large body of work depicting all 21 missions.

This chapter focuses on the work of three painters of exceptional talent who produced images of all the missions, and whose work can be found in several California museums: Henry Chapman Ford, Chris Jorgensen and Edwin Deakin.

Henry Chapman Ford

Henry Chapman Ford published *Etchings of the Franciscan Missions of California* in 1883. In the summers of 1880 and 1881 he had traveled to each mission site by horse and buggy. He made pencil drawings and painted sketches on the mission grounds, then refined the work in his studio in Santa Barbara. Ford was a Civil War illustrator and veteran. He was born in Livonia, NY in 1828. He studied art in Paris and Florence during the late 1850s.

Ford's etchings of the missions have been widely reproduced. His broader body of mission work is not as well known. Ford was the first artist to make a set of mission images in two media, oil and etching. His oil paintings are mostly in private hands although the Bancroft Library at UC Berkeley, the Cantor Arts Center at Stanford University and the Oakland (CA) Museum have representative Ford oils on display.

Ford moved to Chicago after being discharged from the service. He helped found the Academy of Design in that city. He settled in Santa Barbara in 1875, where he spent the rest of his life. Ford's work was exhibited at the Chicago World's Fair in 1893. He died the next year at age 66.

Christian August Jorgensen

Christian August Jorgensen was born in Oslo, Norway on October 7, 1860. Ten-year old Chris and his mother moved to San Francisco in 1870. He was one of the first students at the San Francisco School of Design when it opened in 1874. He later taught at the school. By the mid 1880s, Jorgensen was a successful landscape painter, with a studio on Post Street.

Jorgensen became interested in the missions in the 1880s. For five years he and his wife, Angela, visited all 21 missions. During this period he produced 80 watercolor studies and a complete set of oils.

More than 60 of Jorgensen's mission watercolors (and one oil) were put on display at Mission Sonoma in 1969, where thousands view them each year as they visit Sonoma State Park.

Jorgensen is not only well known for his mission paintings, he became one of the early Yosemite artists. Along with Albert Bierstadt, Thomas Hill, William Smith Jewett and others Jorgensen popularized Yosemite. He built a studio home at Yosemite and painted there every summer for 19 years. His paintings of the missions and Yosemite induced many to visit California, made easier with the completion of the Union Pacific Railroad.

There is representative body of Jorgensen's work at the Huntington Library in San Marino and the Oakland Museum.

Jorgensen enjoyed a long, successful career. He continued to paint until just before his death at his Piedmont (Oakland) family home on June 24, 1935. He was 75 when he died.

Edwin Deakin

Edwin Deakin was born in Sheffield, England on May 21, 1838. He was apprenticed at age 12 to a firm where he was taught to paint landscapes on boxes and tables. He apparently never had any other art training, but this self-taught artist was widely recognized in France and England for his architectural paintings by the time he was 18.

The Deakin family moved to America in 1856, settling in Chicago. Young Edwin exhibited portraits of Civil War heroes at the Chicago Art Academy. In 1865 he married Isabel Fox. Five years later the Deakin relocated to San Francisco. Deakin became a recognized landscape painter, one who focused on historic ruins. Most of his paintings are characterized by detailed renderings of architectural surfaces. He is most famous for the mission paintings he completed between1879-1900. Over a 20-year period, Deakin painted two sets of the missions in oil and one in watercolor.

Deakin's skillful renderings were executed in a style that was characterized as "romantic, picturesque and nostalgic." The missions had a special visual appeal.

Deakin carefully researched each mission so he could accurately recreate how it looked when it was still largely intact. He obtained early drawings and photographs of missions which had been totally destroyed. He used an oil painting by L. Tousset, for example, as a point of reference when he painted Mission Santa Cruz.

In his 1905 article about Deakin, published in *Brush and Pencil*, Robert Hewitt stressed how well the artists' picturesque style fit the mission subject: "It was a happy thought to

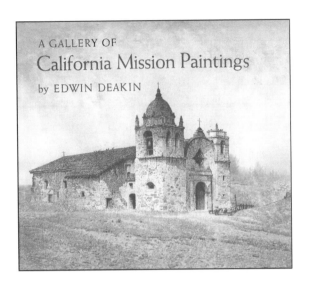

A GALLERY OF
California Mission Paintings
by EDWIN DEAKIN

undertake the task of transmitting to future generations these notable old structures in all their time-worn beauty. . ... It will readily be seen that the interests of the canvas is largely historical, and yet the crumbling condition of many of the structures and their unusual style of architecture lend them an air of the picturesque. The fact that some of these buildings . . . are stained and mellowed by time and crumbling into ruins (help explain why,) the missions were subjects to delight the heart of a true painter."

The working sketches for his mission paintings can be seen in the Howard Willoughby collection in the Oakland Art Museum, which also contains many of his paintings. A complete set of Deakin' large oil paintings of the missions are on display at the Los Angeles County Museum of Natural History. A "gallery" of Deakin paintings was published in 1966.

Deakin traveled and sketched in Europe, occupied a studio in Denver for a few years, finally settling permanently in Berkeley, CA. In 1890, he purchased a large track of land and built a mission-style studio. Deakin worked out of that studio until his death on May 11, 1923, just before he would have turned 85. His wife Isabel was at his side.

REFERENCES:

A Gallery of California Mission Paintings by Edwin Deakin, The Ward Ritchie Press: Los Angeles, 1966.

Romance of the Bells: The California Missions in Art by Jean Stern and Gerald J. Miller,The Irvine Museum: Irvine, CA 1995.

Impressions of California: Early Currents in Art 1850-1930, by The Irvine Museum The Irvine Museum: Irvine, CA 1995.

An Artist Records the California Missions, By Henry Chapman Ford, 1889.

Mission San Luis Obispo

Pioneer photographers documented the state of the missions, several of which suffered from "modernization." This photograph shows the New England steeple added to San Luis Obispo in 1880. It was restored to its original form in 1934.

CHAPTER 25

MISSION PHOTOGRAPHERS

Pioneering masters of the new medium of
photography whose images of the old missions
captivated the general public between 1885-1920

Photography was in its infancy when the mission era
was ending in California. The Frenchman Nicephore
Niepce created the first permanent image in 1826. The
daguerreotype was perfected in 1839. This new medium continued to advance, but until the introduction of the Brownie
in 1900, it was a tool for professional photographers like Carleton E. Watkins, one of the early giants in the field.

In 1854, after relocating to California from New York, the
25-year-old Watkins met a pioneer daguerreotyper, R.H. Vance.
An opening for an operator at Vance's San Jose studio gave
Watkins an opportunity to learn how to coat the daguerreotype plates and make exposures. He showed an instinctive
knack for the medium, and by 1857, had opened up his own
studio, specializing in portraits and view photography. In the
summers he would travel and photograph. He was one of the
first individuals to photograph Yosemite Valley.

In 1880, Watkins went to Southern California for the first
time. On his return he traveled along the El Camino Real Trail
and photographed the old missions.

Watkins images, typically made on a large-view camera,
are the earliest photographic collection of the missions. He
captured many of the missions before their surroundings
were overrun with urban sprawl.

As the camera became more portable, and the medium improved, cameras were increasingly used to record important events. A remarkable 1882 photograph recorded the investigation of the remains of Father Junipero Serra at the Carmel Mission.

Soon, entrepreneurial photographers were taking photographs of mission visitors, hauling equipment to the still remote mission sites by wagon.

Santa Clara Fire

When the technology became more generally available, professional photographers like Adam Clark Vroman often started camera clubs.

Vroman (1856-1916) was an important pioneer photographer. He started work on a complete series of the California missions in 1895. Vroman took many of the earliest available photographs of the church interiors, essential records for later restoration efforts.

After Vroman's death in 1916, all that survived of his work were original glass plate negatives. Between 1961-1972, William Webb made gelatin silver prints from the Vroman negatives. The prints are now in the California Museum of Photography at the University of California, Riverside.

With the growth of photojournalism the camera was increasingly used to capture dramatic events "on the spot." In 1929, when the Mission Santa Clara church burned to the ground, a newspaper photographer was present to record the scene.

Photojournalists also recorded the arrival of famous people at the missions, like then-Senator and Mrs. John F.

Pasadena Camera Club c. 1900 (Vroman on right)

Kennedy, when they visited the Carmel mission.

Professional photographers didn't abandon the missions in the 20th century. For example, Will Connell was an accomplished commercial photographer who specialized in the "Southern California" lifestyle. However, an important personal project of his was to photograph all 21 missions and their asistencias (sub-missions)—a project he completed between 1936-37. He published a book of his mission photos in 1941.

Carleton E. Watkins was the most important photographer to leave a full body of mission images. Watkins is best know for his mammoth plates and stereograph views of Yosemite. His images were so compelling that President Abraham Lincoln signed a bill in 1864, making the valley inviolable, and paving the way for the National Park Service.

Watkins was a lousy and unlucky businessman, however. He had to declare bankruptcy in 1874, and his negatives and gallery prints were sold to Isaiah Taber, who began to publish Watkins' images as his own. Watkins gradually rebuilt his collection. He was in the process of negotiating with Stanford

San Luis Rey

University for his body of work when the 1906 earthquake struck San Francisco. His entire remaining collection was destroyed in the fire that followed the quake.

Watkins was so traumatized by the loss of his life's work that he retired to his small ranch in Yolo County. He was partially blind and in poor health. He eventually was committed to the Napa State Hospital for the insane in 1910. He died on June 23 at the age of 87.

REFERENCES:

Carleton Watkins: From Where the View Looked Best. Published by the J. Paul Getty Museum in cooperation with the Henry E. Huntington Library.

Carleton Watkins: The Art of Perception by Douglas R. Nickel, Maria Morris Hambourg and the San Francisco Museum of Modern Art. Harry N. Abrams, Inc. 1999

Collection of Photographs by Carleton E. Watkins 1874-1890 , University of California, Berkeley. The Watkins Family History Society also provides a selection online http://watkins.org/photos

Dwellers at the Source by William Webb and Robert A. Weinstein contains many of the photographs of Adam Clark Vroman.

The Missions of California, by Will Connell 1941.

Lady by Bell—San Miguel

In 1904, the women of California set out to preserve the historic road that connected the missions, El Camino Real. The road was documented with marker
bells and bell displays were erected at individual missions. The driving force
behind this effort was Mrs. A.S.C. Forbes.

CHAPTER 26

MRS. A.S.C. FORBES

Writer and civic leader who led the effort to
preserve El Camino Real and mark the historic
trail with guidepost bells

As the 19th century came to a close, there was growing public interest in the missions. Edward Vischer's
drawings, published as *The Mission Era* in 1878,
sparked a yearning for the simpler pastoral life shown in his
watercolors. Helen Hunt Jackson's 1882 novel, *Ramona*, made
the Spanish era seem romantic. The California impressionists
featured the missions in their paintings, calling attention to
their crumbling conditions.

By the last decade of the century the public was ready to
take steps to preserve its heritage. Charles Lummis, a newspaperman and Indian activist, argued that the missions had
to be saved. In 1895, Lummis and a group of California's most
prominent leaders founded the Landmarks Club, dedicated to
saving the missions and other historic buildings. A group of
California woman had an equally important idea: Preserve
the "highway" that connected the missions, the 700-mile dirt
road known as El Camino Real. A few years earlier, Anna
Pitcher, a prominent member of the Woman's Club of Los
Angeles, had issued a plea to preserve this historic trail in a
widely reported speech. Over the next decade there was considerable discussion, but no action. It wasn't until 1904 when
a group of women formed the El Camino Real Association.

When Mrs. Armitage Suton Carion Forbes (known as Mrs. A.S.C. Forbes) agreed to serve on the Executive Committee of the new association, everyone knew things would happen.

Forbes had been a prominent member of Los Angeles society since she and her wealthy husband moved to California in 1895. In addition to numerous civic duties, Forbes worked as a freelance reporter and she wrote one of the first guidebooks to Los Angeles, which was published in 1903.

Along with her colleagues in the Camino Real Association, Forbes researched the exact location of the original trail, and raised money for its preservation. Then they came up with a big idea – the creation of a distinctive marker that would capture public attention and help the growing band of motor enthusiasts tour the original road and see the missions and other historic buildings. A competition was held to select the marker. Forbes' entry, building on an idea originally suggested by a friend, was selected. The design combined a 100-pound cast iron bell mounted on an 11-foot shaft, curved to look like a Franciscan walking stick.

The woman's group raised money to pay for the manufacture and placement of about 400 of the guidepost bells between 1906-1913. One was placed in front of each of the missions. Forbes, spurred by her bell research, wrote two books, *Mission Tales in the Days of the Dons* in 1909, and *California Missions and Landmarks* in 1914.

For California, with her Missions old,
Her tales bewitching, and her days of gold,
Her brown-robed padres of the distant past,
Would that the glory of that age might last.
By Anna I. Dempsey, a friend of Mrs. Forbes
❦ Published in *California Missions and Landmarks*

Ever alert to a business opportunity, Forbes' husband acquired a foundry in 1908, and was soon producing most of the El Camino marker bells.

In 1914, the Forbes started another company, the Novelty Manufacturing Co., to produce miniature bells for sale to the public.

The woman who was the driving force in marking El Camino Real was born Harrye Rebecca Piper Smith in Everett, PA,

Mrs. A.S.C. Forbes

May 6, 1861, of Quaker parents. Her family moved to Wichita, KS where she attended a private college in 1883. In 1886, she married Armitage Suton Carion Forbes.

203

Armitage Forbes made his money initially in cattle, and then acquired the Pacific Bottling Works in Tacoma, WA, where he and his bride lived for a few years. In 1891, the Forbes moved to London for three years. He acquired the Blair Camera Co., one of the more successful early camera manufacturers. Forbes sold his company to Kodak in 1897, a couple years after returning to the United States and moving to Los Angeles.

The Forbes' had a successful marriage. Both were dynamic high achievers. While Armitage Forbes concentrated on his business interests, ranging from an orange grove in Glendora to a gold mine in Kern County, his wife was a civic leader and writer. Both were accomplished photographers. Mrs. Forbes, at one point, was a director of the Los Angeles Camera Club and opened the first photographic salon in Los Angeles.

When Armitage Forbes died in 1928, his wife took over running the foundry and the bell business. She and her brother operated this business for 20 more years. She sold the business, which still operates as the California Bell Co. She continued to be active in civic affairs until her health began to fail in 1948. She died Sept. 18, 1951. Over her 90 years, Forbes left her mark on history. Thanks to Forbes, the missions and their ways of life, were brought to the attention of motorists as they cruised California roads. The Forbes bell became an enduring symbol for the missions and their places in California history.

REFERENCES:

California's Spanish Mission by Spencer Crump, Corona de Mar, CA: Trans-Anglo Books, 1975. This book dedicates a chapter to the preservation of the missions.

The website of the California Bell Company www.californiabell.com tells the history of the bell markers and points out where the largest concentration of original bells exists (Paradise Point Resort in San Diego.)

California's El Camino Real and its Historic Bells by Max Kurillo and Erline Tuttle, Sunbelt Publications, 2000. Dedicated to the women who "preserved and marked" El Camino Real, this is the definitive book on the history of the roadside bell markers. It contains a summary of the life of Mrs. A.S.C. Forbes. Several photographs I have used were originally published in this book.

California Missions and Landmarks by Mrs. A.S.C. Forbes, Los Angeles: 1915. An enthusiastic and comprehensive account; contains interesting but small black and white photographs.

THE CAMINO REAL was like a chain that linked together Father (Junipero) Serra's rosary, the missions, about which lingers the memory of a saint and the scent of a rose.

The establishment of the California missions began during the reign of the Spanish bourbon king Carlos III, when he commenced the colonization of the Golden State of California. The highway along which the picturesque civilization center was El Camino Real, the Royal Road, the Kings Highway, the recognized route of official travel when California was part of Spain.

In the 17th century the camino reales of Spain were the envy of the world. They were beautified by trees, enhanced by picturesque ventas, or inns, and enriched with national or memorial monuments. In California . . . in place of ventas, missions were built and the road that joined them was embellished by the unfettered beauties of luxuriant flora and wild vegetation, varied with the silver trail of water-falls, and the deep green-blue of billowy sea.

After founding the second mission . . . orders were given to open up and keep in repair a road for transportation of supplies and for traffic between San Diego and Monterey. As each succeeding mission was established, the duty of maintaining the road fell to those missions that it directly connected. Indians were employed constantly upon the task and were paid from the treasury the same as for other work and were given a home and board at the mission. The Franciscans (never) made the American Camino Real one that compared with those of Spain. Yet in the project to revive the sentiment of the historic road, there is the opportunity to make El Camino Real a scenic highway such as they had in Spain, with long vistas of California's glorious trees, varied by artistic hedges of interesting cacti, and trellises of creeping sweet Castilian roses leading to some memorial monument, fountain or shrine erected to the memory of some discoverer, navigator, Indian or padre.

This would in a manner compensate for the loss of the virgin beauty that must have enveloped California's historic road before civilization began to farm away the charm of the wild.

❦ Mrs. A.S.C. Forbes in *California Missions and Landmarks*, 1815

San Gabriel Mission – c. 1900

*John Steven McGroarty's three-hour musical extravaganza, **The Mission Play**, was performed at a playhouse built near the San Gabriel Mission. The play ran for 21 years.*

CHAPTER 27

JOHN STEVEN McGROARTY

The author of the long-running, *The Mission Play*, a three-hour extravaganza that told the story of the founding, success and ultimate decline of the missions

On April 29, 1912 the movers and shakers of Southern California traveled to a new playhouse built near the old Mission San Gabriel for the first showing of *The Mission Play*. This three-hour extravaganza was a huge success. The three-act play was staged each year for the next two decades, and recreated again in 1936 for the International Exposition held in San Diego. More than 2.5 million people saw the performance during its 21-year run.

The Mission Play told the story of the founding, success and ultimate decline of the old Spanish missions. The central character was Junipero Serra, the Franciscan founder of the first nine missions. The lavish scenery featured two of the most famous and beautiful missions: Mission Carmel (Act II) and San Juan Capistrano (Act III). The play had everything: A heroic story, a sub-plot involving a comely half-blood Indian damsel who Fr. Serra rescues from the clutches of a lustful Spanish Commandante, Indian war dances for the kids, great music and a colorful Fiesta scene that involved almost the entire cast of 300 players: Soldiers, Spanish women with 'brilliant-hued gowns,' picturesque Caballeros, savage chiefs in full regalia and dozens of Indian dancers. The production cost $1.5 million to stage.

John Steven McGroarty

The author of *The Mission Play* was an Irish protestant, John Stephen McGroarty. McGroarty had moved to Los Angeles 10 years earlier at age 40. He had quickly become a prominent state booster. A lawyer turned poet, McGroarty published a column in the Los Angeles Times for 40 years. His Sunday essays reveled in the state's growth, memorialized California history and traditions, provided Emersonian encouragement and often featured his poetry. His 1903 poem *Just California* became required reading for several generations of California schoolchildren. In 1933, after the success of *The Mission Play* and his poems, the state Legislature declared him official Poet Laureate of California, a lifetime appointment.

John Stephen McGroarty was born in Luzerne County, PA on August 20, 1962. After a short term as a teacher he was elected Pennsylvania Justice of the Peace in 1883 at age 21. He was admitted to the bar in 1894, opened a general practice in Wilkes-Barre, and then became a lawyer for Anaconda Copper Mining Co. McGroarty moved to Montana in 1896 to run the Butte Light Co., then invested in a mining venture in Mexico which failed.

In November 1901 he and his wife Ida moved to Los Angeles, where he found his true calling. The publisher of the Los Angeles Times, Harrison Gray Otis hired him as a essayist. In 1906 McGroarty also took became editor of *West Coast Magazine* (a Grafton Publishing Co. monthly that promoted the beauty and great living conditions of Southern California).

McGroarty was an obvious choice then, when Frank Miller, founder of the Mission Inn at Riverside California, decided that California needed something like Germany's Oberammergan Passion Play. The president of Stanford proposed McGroarty as playwright.

In the early decades of the 20th century there were a number of outdoor drama-pageants, including a Ramona Pageant at Hemet and the Pasadena Festival of Roses. *The Mission Play* outdrew them all. The production was well financed. The tycoon Henry Huntington helped underwrite the expensive production. An umbrella organization, the Mission Play Association was formed, and built a special 1,450-seat playhouse for the play. The playhouse had a giant pipe organ that was, by all accounts a wonder to hear.

The play dialogue was quite flowery, as is McGroarty's poetry. Kevin Starr, the California state librarian, calls McGroarty "a genial journalist and a dream poet of the lo! Hark! School." There is a famous scene in the play where Padre Serra defies the powerful commandante. His speech is typical of the sententious dialogue "If you shall but so much as touch this young creature with your vile polluting hands, upon you head shall I hurl the curse of the church." In modern terms the play was politically incorrect. McGroarty admired the Franciscans for the job they did to "take an idle race and put it to work—a useless race that they made useful in the world" and the Indians are portrayed as subservient, indolent creatures.

Nonetheless, *The Mission Play* was a well-staged, fast-paced spectacle and it became a California institution.

McGroarty himself was a celebrity. He was twice elected to the U.S. Congress (1934-37). He was a colorful figure and an effective advocate, best known as a champion of the Townsend Plan, a proposal to give $200 a month to pensioners. This ultimately led to the establishment of the Social Security system.

McGroarty, a Democrat who supported Franklin Roosevelt's New Deal, broke with the president over his packing of the Supreme Court. He did not seek re-election after his second term. While he flirted with politics in the following years he effectively retired to his ranch where he was known as the "Sage of Verdugo Hills."

Congressman McGroarty was re-introduced to a new generation of Americans in 1956 when then-Senator John F. Kennedy quoted from one of his letters in *Profiles in Courage*. McGroarty had been in Congress just two months when a constituent demanded to know what he had done to have the Sierra Madre Mountains reforested, and apparently complained that they still didn't look green. He wrote back complaining that "One of the countless drawbacks of being in Congress is that I am compelled to receive impertinent letters from a jackass like you. Will you please take two running jumps and go to hell."

John Stephen McGroarty died at St. Vincent's Hospital on August 7, 1944. His wife of 50 years had passed away several years earlier. McGroarty, who had converted to Catholicism late in life, was honored at a High Mass presided over by the Archbishop of Los Angeles. His ranch was ultimately sold to the city and is now the John Steven McGroarty Memorial Archive Library. It was declared an historic monument in 1970.

McGroarty's *The Mission Play* helped give a land of newcomers like himself a respectable history. As Kevin Starr said eloquently, McGroarty "provided Southern California with a usable past, a revered founding time, at once escapist and assuring, linking a parvenu society with the rich ecclesiastical cultures of Mediterranean Europe."

THE KING'S HIGHWAY

All in the golden weather forth let us ride today,
You and I together on the King's Highway,
The blue skies above us, and below the shining sea,
There's many a road to travel, but it's this road for me.

It's a long road and sunny and the fairest in the world –
There are peaks that rise above it in their snowy mantles curled,
And it leads from the mountains through a hedge of chaparral
Down to the waters where the seagulls call.

It's a long road and sunny, 'tis a long road and old,
And the brown padres made it for the flocks of the fold;
They made it for the sandals of the sinner-folk that trod
From the fields in the open to the shelter house of God.

They made it for the sandals of the sinner folk of old;
Now the flocks they are scattered and death keeps the fold;
But you and I together we will take the road today
With the breath in our nostrils on the King's Highway.

We will take the road together through the morning's golden glow,
And we'll dream of those who trod it in the mellowed long ago;
We will stop at the Missions where the sleeping Padres lay,
And bend a knee above them for their souls' sake to pray.

We'll ride through the valleys where the blossom's on the tree,
Through the orchards and the meadows with the bird and the bee,
And we'll take the rising hills where the manzanitas grow,
Past the gray tails of waterfalls where blue violets blow.

Old conquistadores, O brown priests and all,
Give us your ghosts for company when night begins to fall;
There's many a road to travel, but it's this road today,
With the breath of God about us on the King's Highway.

❧ John Steven McGroarty

The Mission Playhouse
Source: Historic Postcard in Author's Collection

The Mission Playhouse was constructed specifically for the staging of 'The Mission Play,' with funds raised by influential Los Angeles business-men. The overall design was patterned after Mission San Antonio de Padua. The Great Depression put a stop to performances in 1930s. After World War II the city of San Gabriel purchased the playhouse and there was a short-lived attempt to revive the play, but interest in the mission era had waned. The playhouse now functions as the San Gabriel Civic Auditorium.

One thinks that John Steven McGroarty, a populist, would be pleased.

REFERENCES:

"Obituary of John S. McGroarty, California Poet" *New York Times,* August 8, 1944.

"John Steven McGroarty: A Biographical Sketch", by Ed Stephan http://www.ac.wwu.edu/-stephan/jsmbiography.html. A loving remembrance of McGroarty by his nephew.

Profiles in Courage by John F. Kennedy, 1956. Quotes McGroarty in the discussion of pressures which discourage political courage among congressmen and senators.

Just California and Other Poems by John Steven McGroarty, Times-Mirror Press: Los Angeles, 1933.

Inventing the Dream: California through the Progressive Era by Kevin Starr: Oxford University Press, 1985.

Ceremony at San Antonio de Padua Mission

The photograph is of Governor Earl Warren of California at a dedication
ceremony at San Antonio de Padua, restored with funds provided by William
Randolph Hearst.

CHAPTER 28

WILLIAM RANDOLPH HEARST

Newspaper magnate who was a generous
contributor to the missions throughout his
long, controversial life

As Gaspar de Portola marched 350 miles up the California coast to Monterey in 1769, he took note of promising sites for future missions. The plans for the
settlement of Alta California was to locate presidios in San
Diego and Monterey, then add missions along the coast. Portola was particularly taken with a pleasant, heavily forested
valley some 65 miles southeast of Monterey. The Spanish
named it Los Robles—Valley of the Oaks. Two years later,
Junipero Serra accompanied by two other padres, and a small
party, traveled to this site to found the third mission in Alta
California.

Today, Mission San Antonio de Padua sits serenely in a
valley that is little changed over the past 200 years. Gnarled
oak trees and tall willows dot the untouched hillsides. The
population of the area is less than it was in 1800. The mission
itself was painstakingly and fully restored in stages between
1907-1948, and is still operated by the Franciscans. San Antonio de Padua offers visitors a unique opportunity to visit an
authentic mission in a setting that is almost identical to the
landscape Portola and Serra saw during their visits more than
two centuries ago.

The man responsible for the good fortune at Mission San
Antonio de Padua was William Randolph Hearst.

Hearst was one of the most powerful men in America for 50 years. After he persuaded his rich father to let him run the *San Francisco Examiner* when he was only 22, in 1887, Hearst used the paper as the basis of the first multi-media publishing empire. Ultimately, Hearst Corp. would own 28 newspapers, 18 magazines and have virtual control over cartoon syndication. Hearst was the first newspaper tycoon to enter radio; he was the first to create movie newsreels. In a later phase of his life, he produced more than 100 movies and was himself the inspiration for Orson Wells' film, *Citizen Kane*.

For a time, around the turn of the century, Hearst heavily influenced U.S. foreign policy, supporting the Cuban Revolution of 1895 and encouraging war with Spain. Throughout his life he despised "those lazy pot-smoking Spaniards and Mexicans." When an explosion sank the U.S.S. Maine in Havana Harbor, Feb. 15,1898, the Hearst papers ran the headline: War? Sure . . . His aggressive, on-the-scene coverage of the ensuing conflict changed the way journalism would cover major events. One of his reporters, James Creelman, actually led an assault on a blockhouse and was wounded. Hearst, on the scene, reportedly knelt beside Creelman and said, "I'm sorry you're hurt. But wasn't it a splendid flight. We beat every paper in the world!"

Hearst married Millicent Wilson in 1903, ultimately fathering five sons, all of whom would enter the business. He developed political ambitions, and served in the U.S. Congress from 1903-07, but turned his considerable energy elsewhere after being defeated in runs for mayor of New York City and governor of New York.

Events leading to the preservation of San Antonio de Padua started during the first decade of 20th century when Hearst was still living in the East. The last resident pastor had died in 1882, and the church roof collapsed in 1900. Restoration efforts by the California Landmarks League, the Daughters of California Pioneers and the Native Sons of the Golden West helped restore the church itself, in 1907, but the rest of the mission continued to deteriorate. The mission grounds consisted of less than 30 acres, with all the surrounding land in private hands.

William Randolph Hearst

Heart's journey back west began in 1916 when he attended a production of the Ziegfield Follies on Broadway, and became infatuated with a 20-year-old dancer named Marion Davies. Legend has it that he reserved two seats (one for himself, one for his hat) every evening for the next two months. He soon began a long-term love affair with Davies. He and Davies moved to California. He formed Cosmopolitan Productions to produce movies (many starring Davies). He made deals with Paramount, MGM, Warner Brothers and 20th Century Fox to produce and release his films.

217

In 1919, Hearst began planning what would become a 28-year endeavor to build a grand European style castle in the Santa Lucia Mountains, along the California coast, north of Cambria. Excavation for San Simeon began in 1922. The building was not ready for full-time occupancy until 1927. Additions continued until 1947, by which point San Simeon had 130 rooms and a vast collection of antiques and art.

As work on San Simeon progressed slowly in 1920s, Hearst bought more land in the Santa Lucia mountains, including all of the land surrounding San Antonio de Padua—154,000 acres of the most picturesque land in the Valley of the Oaks. He had his San Simeon architect, Julia Morgan, create a hacienda-style "hunting lodge" and working ranch house in the peaceful valley, sited about a half mile from the old mission. Then, he

San Simeon

built a private road between his hacienda and San Simeon, some 15 miles away.

Mission San Antonio de Padua was returned to the Franciscans in 1928 and a new effort begun to restore "the largest and most picturesque of the remaining missions in northern California." A Patron's Day celebration was held each June 13 (the feast day of St. Anthony.) The original church bulto which had been cared for by the Diaz family was returned to the chapel. Hearst contributed funds for the mission's upkeep. He donated 20 acres of land to the mission in 1939 and encouraged planning for a major restoration.

218

World War II delayed restoration, but in 1948, the Franciscans unveiled a bold plan to rebuild the original quadrangle. Seed funds for the project came from a $500,000 donation by the Hearst Foundation for mission restoration, 10 percent of which was earmarked for the rebuilding of San Antonio de Padua.

While the gifts of land and money were crucial, Hearst's biggest contribution may have been how he disposed of his San Lucia holdings. In September 1940 he sold all of his Valley of the Oaks land to the government, which created the Hunter-Liggett Military Reservation there, thus protecting the area from the development and urban crawl that encroached upon so many of the old Spanish missions.

Hearst lived with Davies at San Simeon until 1947, when, in failing health, he moved to Beverly Hills. He and his wife, Millicent, never divorced although it was discussed. Davies, a rare person of uncommon generosity and loyalty, stayed with Hearst until he died August 14, 1951 at age of 88.

Hearst Castle is now a State Historical Monument, run by the California Park Service. His former hunting lodge was turned into a small picturesque hotel, The Hacienda. Both the hotel and Mission San Antonio de Padua are inside the Fort Hunter-Liggett Military Reservation.

Marion Davies dictated her reminisces of her life with Hearst, and this memoir was published as *The Times We Had: Life with William Randolph Hearst*. Marion Davies died on September 22, 1961.

The Hearst Foundation continues to support the missions and is a major contributor to a new initiative by the California Missions Foundation to raise $50 million to fund mission preservation in 21st century.

219

I AM PLEASED TO LEND MY SUPPORT to this campaign because of my interest in California history, as well as my family's long involvement in mission preservation. Phoebe Apperson Hearst was a life member of the Landmarks Club founded by newspaperman Charles Fletcher Lummis. That organization was responsible for saving many of the missions from ruin in the late 1800s. William Randolph Hearst personally contributed to the restoration of many of the missions. Over the years, the Hearst Foundation has significantly funded mission preservation projects, including those at San Antonio de Padua, San Juan Bautista and La Purísima.

It is a privilege to chair the California Missions Foundation "Missions 2000" Campaign, a $50-million initiative to fund ongoing preservation efforts of the 21 historic California missions.

We are at a pivotal point in mission history and begin our campaign at a critical time. Many of the missions are experiencing structural problems and other deteriorating conditions. Projects including seismic retrofitting, and the restoration and preservation of mission artifacts are crucial. In addition, archaeological studies, adobe stabilization, and mission garden renovation and revitalization must be addressed. The growing lists of deferred maintenance and repairs are costly and present ongoing financial challenges.

The California Missions Foundation has committed to taking the lead in this statewide campaign to ensure that the rich legacy of mission history is preserved for future generations. Your generous support is greatly appreciated.

❧ Letter of Stephen Hearst, Chairman, California Missions Foundation

REFERENCES:

The Chief: The Life of William Randolph Hearst by David Nasaw, Houghton Mifflin Co., 2000 Definitive recent biography.

The Times We Had: Life with William Randolph Hearst, by Marion Davies. Bobbs Merill: Indianopolis, 1975.

Hearst Castle: Biography of a Country House, by Victoria Kastner, Victoria Garagliano (photographer) and George Plimpton. Harry N. Abrams Co., 2000. Comprehensive, lavishly illustrated.

Sarcophagus at Mission Carmel

Since its unveiling in 1924 the sarcophagus created by the sculptor Jo Mora has been one of the most popular attractions at Mission Carmel.

CHAPTER 29

JOSEPH JACINTO – "JO" MORA

The sculptor who created the sarcophagus of
Junipero Serra at Mission Carmel

P resident James Buchanan returned Mission San Carlos Borromeo de Carmelo to the Catholic Church on Oct. 19, 1859. The roof of the church had collapsed in 1851, and the rest of the buildings were in ruins. While services were periodically held in the sacristy, which was largely intact, there wasn't a serious effort made to restore the mission church until 1882.

Heading the restoration effort was Father Angelo D. Cassanova, pastor of the Catholic Church in Monterey, who solicited funds for the project. The debris that had accumulated in the church interior was removed and the church was roofed. Unfortunately, the new shingled roof was steeply pitched and incompatible with the church's overall design. Despite criticism over the appearance, the roof protected the church for the next 52 years until master restorer Harry Downie replaced it.

Despite periodic talk about the need to fully restore the Carmel mission, nothing more was done for almost 40 years. In 1919, a new pastor, Father Ramon Mestres, started an archaeological excavation in the fields around the church to pinpoint the foundations of the original quadrangle. He also set up a restoration fund in 1920. To give the restoration effort a focus, Mestres commissioned the noted artist, Jo

Mora, to design a memorial sculpture to honor Father Junipero Serra. Mora had just been discharged from the U.S. Army, where he was a major of field artillery during World War I.

Mora was no stranger to the mission. He had toured the Monterey peninsula in 1907. A visit to the Carmel mission that year inspired him to visit and sketch all the missions.

I AM HERE (in San Francisco) to settle up one of the most important and interesting commissions I have ever been given. It is to execute the Sarcophagus for Father Junipero Serra and the three Franciscans buried beside him in Mission Carmel. Could anything be grander for a sculptor who loves his California – or fraught with more romantic and sentimental possibilities? I'm girding my loins for the supreme professional effort of my life.

💐 Letter from Jo Mora to Senator James Phelan, Dec. 10, 1920

Mestres' plan was to rebuild one of the original rooms, adjacent to the church, and exhibit the Mora piece and some art from the original mission, to attract more visitors and stimulate further restoration.

Mora's proposed that the work be a large sarcophagus. It would show a recumbent Serra on his deathbed, surrounded by three other early Franciscan missionaries. There was some objection to the original design since the padre who was to stand grieving at Serra's head, Father Juan Crespi, had died before Serra. However, artistic license prevailed and the original design was approved. Crespi was, in fact, a brilliant choice. He was a close friend of Serra's with whom he had studied philosophy years earlier in Palma. Crespi served with Serra at the Serra Gorda and Baja missions. He was one of the first padres recruited to colonize California. He was the official chaplain and diarist for the 1769 expedition that founded Alta California.

The Serra sarcophagus was unveiled Oct. 12, 1924 in the reconstructed wing and small chapel, just off the mission church.

The sarcophagus, features life-size figures on an 8-foot by 12-foot travertine and bronze base. Technically the sculpture is a cenotaph, since the remains of the Franciscans are buried in the church sanctuary. Ever since it was unveiled in 1924, the memorial that

Joseph Jacinto —"Jo" Mora

Mora created has been one of the most popular attractions at Mission Carmel.

Joseph Jacinto Mora, a friendly man who liked to be called "Jo," was born in Montevideo, Uruguay on Oct. 22, 1876. After his family moved to the United States he attended Pingry Academy in Elizabeth, NJ, graduating in 1894. His father, who came from Catalonia, Spain, was a sculptor, and young Mora studied with him for a time. His mother was French, from Alsace Lorraine. Mora studied art at the American Students League in Boston and the Chase School. While in Boston he worked as a cartoonist at the *Boston Herald.* Mora also won contracts to write and illustrate books based on the old classics.

While he had a promising career in front of him, Mora felt constrained by this traditional life, and he decided to move out West. He traveled by horseback to San Jose, CA, working at ranches along the way. Between 1904 and 1907 he lived with the Hopi and Navajo Indians in Arizona and New Mexico. He learned the Navajo language so well he was used as a translator during his army service. Mora took what turned out to be the last photograph of the Hopi religious ceremonies, so invaluable that it now is at the Smithsonian Institution.

Mora returned to California in 1907 and married Grace Needham. The couple settled in Mountain View, CA. Mora's reputation grew. During this period he was primarily known as a cowboy artist. He and his family moved to Carmel in 1922 when he received the Serra commission. He lived there the rest of his life.

Mora was an incredibly versatile artist: a painter, illustrator, muralist and sculptor. He also wrote and illustrated children's books, and was an accomplished photographer. Mora created a 100-foot long diorama of the Portola expedition for the Golden Gate International Exposition in 1929. He was also commissioned to draw 13 biographical murals for the Will Rogers Memorial in Claremont OK. His sculptures appear all over California: mounted figures at the U.S. Navy Postgraduate School, a monument to Cervantes in Golden Gate Park in San Francisco and a statue of Bret Harte at the Bohemian Club, also in San Francisco. The list of his "major" work is extensive.

Mora became a popular figure in Carmel, best known for the whimsical maps he created and had reproduced for sale to the general public. These accurate, but fanciful maps that he called cartes, depicted California, Yosemite, Yellowstone and the Grand Canyon. They are now collector's items.

Along with his many other talents, Mora was an accomplished writer. He published three books: *Log of the Spanish Main,* in 1933, *Trail Dust and Saddle Leather,* in 1946, and *Californios* in 1949, a book that celebrated the vaqueros who worked the cattle ranches in California in the days of Mexican rule.

There was a major retrospective of exhibition of Mora at the Monterey Museum of Art in 1998. The museum produced a book *Jo Mora: Artist and Writer* and a map showing the location of his works in public places. Both publications are still available. The Monterey History and Art Association and the Harrison Memorial Library in Carmel both have extensive Mora holdings.

Mora continued to work until his health began failing in 1946. He died Oct. 10, 1947 at age 71.

REFERENCES:

Jo Mora, Renaissance Man of the West, by Stephen Mitchell, Stoecklein Publishers, 1994.

"Old West Preserved in Jo Mora's Work" by John Woolfenden in *Monterey Herald,* March 10, 1973 A comprehensive article

Trail Dust and Saddle Leather by Jo Mora, Charles Scribner & Sons: New York, 1946.

Californios by Jo Mora, published after his death in 1949, Charles Scribner & Co. Inc., Garden City, NY.

Jo Mora: Artist and Writer, Monterey Museum of Art: Monterey CA, 1998. Contains well executed photographs and scans of Mora's work, printed on glossy paper

Mission Carmel Church c. 1920

One of the first projects undertaken by the Master Restorer Harry Downie was to replace the steep shingled roof of Mission Carmel (added in 1884) with a more authentic, curved roof.

CHAPTER 30

HARRY DOWNIE

The gifted artisan and master mission restorer who
dedicated 50 years of his life to the restoration of
Mission Carmel and led the drive for the authentic
restoration of these unique treasures

It was a bitter cold day in 1931 when the 28-year-old cabinetmaker stopped off to visit Monsignor Philip Scher,
pastor of the Catholic Church in Monterey. Scher had
admired the artisan's skillful restoration of a fire-damaged
altar at Santa Clara University, and the two men had become
friends. The man, Henry John Downie, who everyone called
Harry, intended to stay just for a few days to restore an old
statue at the Carmel mission. He stayed 50 years.

Over the next five decades, Downie carefully guided the
restoration of San Carlos Borromeo de Carmelo, the most
beautiful of the old Spanish missions of Alta California. In
1931, much of the mission was in poor condition. The church
was intact, but a pitched shingle roof added in 1884 marred
its once-graceful roofline. In short, full restoration of Mission
Carmel, as it was popularly called, was an enormous task.

Initially, Downie was given religious objects to restore,
but his role quickly broadened to mission restorer. By early
1932, Downie was officially designated as curator at Mission
Carmel. Thus began what would be a decades long process of
restoration of the historic mission. In the early years he did
much of the work himself, living in a room which is now the
restored mission library.

By the end of 1936, Downie had returned the roof to its original lines and part of one wing was rebuilt. Gradually the entire site of the original mission was excavated. In 1939, in the course of one dig, Downie discovered fragments of the original cross erected by Father Junipero Serra in 1771. Downie had a replica built there, near the edge of the mission quadrangle.

After 20 years, the exterior restoration of Mission Carmel was substantially completed and Downie went back into his workshop to carve the reredos and a pulpit for the church. He completed these tasks in 1956-57. During his stay at the mission, he also served as the church bell ringer, a post he held for 43 years.

> RESTORING THE WALLS
>
> You start with what you find and continue in the same way. You have to do it the way they did, putting in all the crooked walls and inaccuracies. If you follow your own ideas, you'll fizzle.
>
> ๖ Harry Downie (regarding his views on the correct approach to restoration)

Over the years Downie's reputation as a master restorer and the preeminent expert on the California missions grew. He was consulted on, and helped restore, many of the missions that are today considered the most authentic. He guided the restorations of San Luis Obispo, San Juan Bautista and San Buenaventura – all three defaced by "modernization." He assisted the Native Daughters of the Golden West in the rebuilding of Mission Soledad between 1954 and 1963. He also helped in the painstaking restoration of San Antonio de Padua, which began in 1948 with a grant from the Hearst Foundation. Here the ruins of all the buildings, except for the church, were removed. New adobe bricks were made from the remnants of the original walls, and the entire quadrangle restored.

Right up until his death, in 1980, Downie was passionately involved in mission restoration. Just before he died he was consulting on the planned renovation of Mission San Jose.

Who was Harry Downie?

Henry John Downie was a third generation San Franciscan. He was born of Irish and Scott parents on August 25, 1903, and

Downie in his workshop

grew up in San Francisco. The family was Catholic, and their parish was Mission Dolores, located three blocks south of Market Street, between 16th and 17th streets. As a boy Downie was artistic. By the age of 12 he had carved his first model . . . of Mission Dolores. He was intimately familiar with the ruins of the Carmel mission. His family vacationed in Carmel each summer and Downie often recalled wandering among the ruins of the old stone church as a boy.

231

Downie became a cabinetmaker, and opened up shop in San Francisco in the late 1920s. He quickly developed a reputation for his superb restorations of Spanish antiques. However, the great depression was tough on all small businesses and by 1931 he decided to relocate to Santa Barbara, where he had the promise of new work.

Downie became the driving force in the restoration of Mission Carmel. In the early years, before he was married, he lived at the mission. He would often wear a Franciscan habit. Most days he could be seen at the mission, removing layers of broken roof tiles, pinpointing the location of old walls, or cleaning an original statue someone had discovered. The restoration was privately funded, and the former cabinetmaker was frugal, yet creative. Timbers for the new roof came from a grandstand erected in 1834 for a pageant honoring Fr. Serra.

Downie with priest

Downie was a hands-on artisan. When the funds were available to restore the mission roof to its original style, he built the unique curved supports in his workshop. He carved many of the artifacts that visitors admire, but only after painstaking research into the originals of the period. His crowning accomplishments as a master carver were the reredos and pulpit in the mission church, which he completed in 1956-57.

232

When Downie met his future wife, Mabel, he moved out of

THE THING THAT PLEASES ME (when watching tourists at Mission Carmel) is that they don't just take pictures of the façade or of the quadrangle, but that they find interesting little details all over the place on which to train their lenses. Those details are as authentic as I could make them.

🦋 Harry Downie

the mission. He and his wife had two daughters, Miriam and Ann Marie.

Downie was honored in the later years of his life as the scope and quality of what he had accomplished became more widely known. In 1954, Pope Pius XII appointed Downie a Knight of St. Gregory. In 1968, he was presented with an Award of Merit by the California Historic Society for his work in mission restoration and named Man of the Year by the Monterey Chamber of Commerce. Downie was made an honorary citizen of Petra, (Junipero Serra's birthplace) and received Spain's Medal of Honor. Throughout it all, what really motivated him was a new discovery, or a new challenge, that would advance the authentic restoration of the missions of Alta California.

Harry Downie died on March 10, 1980, in Carmel, CA. He and his wife are buried alongside the church of San Carlos Borromeo de Carmelo, where he can keep watch on any future restoration of the mission he served so faithfully for 50 years.

Older Downie

ALL THE WORK I HAVE DONE here has been with the idea of creating a fitting memorial to Junipero Serra, the Apostle of California.

🦋 Harry Downie

REFERENCES:

"Mission Models Were Harry Downie's Hobby," *Monterey Peninsula Herald,* June 1, 1970.

"Harry Downie—Man of the Year", by Everett Mesick, *Monterey Peninsula Herald,* January 14, 1969.

"Obituary of Harry Downie", *Monterey Peninsula Herald,* March 10, 1980.

"He Brings History to Life", by Judith A. Eisner, *The Pine Cone,* August 24, 1972.

IMAGE SOURCES AND CREDITS

Cover and inside photograph of San Fernando Rey Convento by David J. McLaughlin © Pentacle Press 2003.

Introduction
- Mission Carmel c. 1895 by George Fiske, from Pat Hathaway Collection.

Chapter 1 – Juan Cabrillo
- Monterey Presidio, a 1856 drawing by Henry Miller reproduced in *California Missions: The Earliest Series of Views*.
- Engraving of Cabrillo is by Armandina Lozano.

Chapter 2 – Gaspar de Portola
- First mass at Monterey. Copy of 1877 oil by Leon Trousset, recreating the event.
- Original of Gaspar de Portola portrait appears in the Paradort National de Turisimo of Arties, Spain. Reproduced in the book *Gaspar de Portola, Explorer and Founder of California*, translated and revised by Alan K. Brown, Lerida, 1983.

Chapter 3 – Junipero Serra
- Cloister of San Francisco de Palma from *Junipero Serra: A Pictorial Biography* by Martin J. Morgado.
- The "Queretaro Serra Portrait" was painted by Fr. Jose Mosqueda. This 26' by 20' oil is believed to have been done in 1773 when Serra returned to Mexico City. A copy exists at Mission Santa Barbara Archive Library.

Chapter 4 – Juan Bautista de Anza
- This 1832 rendering of San Gabriel was done by Ferdinand Deppe, a German living in Mexico. It is the oldest known oil painting of a California mission.
- Etching of Juan Bautista de Anza, National Park Service.

Chapter 5 – Philipe de Neve
- Image of cannon being fired was taken at 2001 Presidio Days at Santa Barbara, courtesy of Michael Hardwick.
- Michael Hardwick as Philipe de Neve, courtesy of Michael Hardwick.

Chapter 6 – Pedro Yanunali
- Chumash Indians in plank canoe is from a large mural done in 1992 by Robert Thomas and a team of artists; photograph courtesy of Michael Hardwick.
- Pedro Yanunali's home is a rendering done by Clarence Cullimore, published in *Santa Barbara Adobes*.

Chapter 7 – Francisco Hermenegildo Garces
- Franciscan with neophyte by David J. McLaughlin © Pentacle Press 2003.
- Painting of the martyrs Frs. Francisco Garces and Juan Antonio Barreneche is from John Kessell's book *Priests, Soldiers and Reformers*.

Chapter 8 – Manuel Ruiz and Estavan Munras
- Mission Carmel by Clarence Watkins c. 1895, courtesy of Pat Hathaway Collection.
- Royal Presidio Chapel at Monterey by David J. McLaughlin © Pentacle Press 2003.

Chapter 9 – Nikolai Petrovich Rezanov
- Mission Dolores in late 19th century, courtesy of Pat Hathaway Collection.
- Oil painting of Rezanov is in the State Hermitage Museum in St. Petersburg.

Chapter 10 – Hipolite Bouchard
- Painting Attack on Monterey is by Emilio Biggari and hangs in Estudios Historicos Navales de la Armada in Buenos Aires, Argentina. It is reproduced on the cover of Peter Uhrowiczik's book, *The Burning of Monterey*.
- Photograph of the bust of Hipolite Bouchard appears in Carlos Lopez's article "Hipolite Bouchard: Pirate or Patriot" in *Mains Hull Magazine*.

Chapter 11 – Filipe Arroyo de la Cuesta
- Image of Chapel of Cieneguitas and Kaswa village is a reproduction of a painting done by Henry S. Ford in 1930s.
- Mission San Juan Bautista, a 1856 drawing by Henry Miller, reproduced in *California Missions: The Earliest Series of Views.*

Chapter 12 – Estanislao
- Soldiers Barracks, an original photograph by David J. McLaughlin, © Pentacle Press 2003.
- Statue of "Chief" Stanislaus is by Betty Saletta. It is located in Modesto, California.

Chapter 13 – Mariano Guadalupe Vallejo
- Mission San Francisco Solano, courtesy of Pat Hathaway Collection
- Oil painting of Vallejo by Leonardo Barbieri

Chapter 14 – William Edward Petty Hartnell
- Indian Women is a photograph of a mural that appears in the museum at Mission San Luis Obispo
- Oil painting of Hartnell by Leonardo Barbieri. Original hangs in Library of Hartnell College in Salinas, CA.

Chapter 15 – Auguste Duhaut-Cilly
- View from Ruins of Mission Mill, by David J. McLaughlin © Pentacle Press 2003
- Image of Duhaut-Cilly from the 1999 edition of his journal, published by the University of California

Chapter 16 – Jedediah Strong Smith
- San Luis Rey Mission, a contemporary photograph by David J. McLaughlin, © Pentacle Press 2003
- Statue of Jedediah Smith is by Victor Issa. It was completed in 1992; located at the Civic Center in San Dimas, California.

Chapter 17 – Richard Henry Dana
- Hides Curing in the Sun by David J. McLaughlin, © Pentacle Press 2003
- Image of Dana as a young man, original artist unknown. This has been widely reproduced. A high quality reprint is available from the San Diego Historical Society Photo Gallery.

Chapter 18 – Narciso Duran
- Mission Santa Barbara c. 1890, photographer unknown, courtesy of Pat Hathaway Collection
- Mission San Jose by Edward Vischer, dated August 16, 1866. Originals appear in several collections including the Bancroft Library at University of California, Berkeley and the Honnold Library at Claremont College

Chapter 19 – Antonio Aguirre
- San Juan Capistrano ruins, courtesy of Pat Hathaway Collection.
- Image of Don Antonio Aguirre appeared in an article by Mary H. Haggland, published by *Journal of San Diego History*.

Chapter 20 – Pio Pico
- Pico House, downtown Los Angeles. Photographer unknown.
- Pio Pico in c. 1845 by Butterfield and Summers

Chapter 21 – John Charles Fremont
- Bear Flag Monument by David J. McLaughlin, © Pentacle Press 2003
- Fremont as a Major General from an article "John Fremont: 1813-1890" edited by A.C. Image at http://www.johnfremont.com

Chapter 22 – Charles Fletcher Lummis
- San Antonio de Padua Ruins, courtesy of Pat Hathaway Collection
- Photograph of Lummis from *The Curious Life of Charles Fletcher Lummis and the Rediscovery of the Southwest* by Mark Thompson

Chapter 23 – Helen Hunt Jackson
- Santa Inez Mission c. 1900, courtesy Pat Hathaway Collection
- Photograph of Helen Jackson is from the American Literature Sites and available online at http://socialhistory.org/Biographies/hhjackson.htm

Chapter 24 – Mission Painters
- The Edwin Deakin painting of San Rafael is from *A Gallery of Mission Paintings* by Edwin Deakin, the front cover of which (also shown) is Deakin's image of the Carmel Mission with the steeply pitched roof which was replaced in 1935-36 by Harry Downie

Chapter 25 – Mission Photographers
- Mission San Luis Obispo, courtesy Pat Hathaway Collection
- Photograph of Santa Clara Mission Church burning is from archives of Santa Clara University
- Photograph of Pasadena Camera Club at San Juan Capistrano is by Victor Clark Vroom, shown in *California's Spanish Missions* by Spencer Crump.
- Photograph of San Fernando Rey is by Clarence Watkins, from author's collection.

Chapter 26 – Mrs. A.S.C. Forbes
- Lady and bell at San Miguel, c. 1915, from Pat Hathaway Collection.
- Photographs of Mrs. A.S.C. Forbes from *California's El Camino Real and its Historic Bells* by Max Urillo and Erline Tuttle.

Chapter 27 – John Steven McGroarty
- San Gabriel c. 1900, by Clarence Watkins, author's collection.
- The photograph of McGroarty is from the online biographical sketch published by his nephew, Ed Stephan, http://www.ac.wwu.edu/-stephan/jsm/biogrpahy.html

Chapter 28 – William Randolph Hearst
- Ceremony at San Antonio de Padua, photographer unknown, courtesy Pat Hathaway Collection.
- Photograph of William Randolph Hearst from *The Chief: The Life of William Randolph Hearst* by David Nasaw.
- Photograph of San Simeon is from *The Biography of a Country House* and the San Simeon website http://www.hearstcastle.org/welcome.asp.
- Book Cover of *The Times We Had: Life with William Randolph Hearst* by Marion Davies is from paperback version, which is still in print.

Chapter 29 – Joseph Jacinto 'Jo' Mora
- Sarcophagus at Mission Carmel by David J. McLaughlin
  © Pentacle Press 2003
- Mora with Serra Sarcophagus c. 1924 courtesy of
  Pat Hathaway Collection.

Chapter 30 – Harry Downie
- Carmel Mission c. 1920s is from the Pat Hathaway Collection
- The photographs of Downie in his workshop in 1941 and in the
  courtyard of Mission Carmel in 1977 originally appeared in the
  Monterey Peninsula Herald.
- Downie by a Restored Wall is from the Pat Hathaway
  Collection

Final Image
- Beatification Ceremony 1988, appeared in *L' Osservatore
  Romano,* Weekly Edition of 24 October,1988.

Beatification of Junipero Serra

Beatification is the next to last step in the path to sainthood. Junipero Serra was declared "Blessed" by Pope John Paul II. This photograph depicts the official ceremony held in Rome on September 25, 1988.

CALIFORNIA MISSIONS GLOSSARY

Many words and phrases used during the mission era are still in use. These include architectural and military terms, religious words and phrases, Native American terms and place names, and of course, the Spanish words for many aspects of everyday life. Some of these terms are technical and rarely used except by experts; others are in more common use. This glossary provides a handy single reference of these terms.

Adobe: Sun-dried bricks made of clay mixed with straw and sometimes horse manure, then baked in the sun. Also refers to structures made of this material.

Aguardiete: A term derived from the Latin *aqua ardens,* which means fiery water. In the mission era aguardiete meant distilled spirits made from the wine of the Mission Grape.

Alcalde: In Spain, a local magistrate. In Alta California, the neophytes appointed to assist the padres in keeping order, reinforcing the rules of the mission and settling minor disputes. They functioned more as policemen than judges.

Alferez: Lowest rank of a commissioned officer in the Spanish Army, equivalent in rank to an ensign or second lieutenant.

Almud: A unit of dry measure representing about 4.2 quarts. It was 1/12 of a fanega.

Alpechin: The mixture of oil and water after pressing olives for oil.

Alta: Upper as in Alta California, the Spanish territory that included present-day California.

Americano: Citizen or resident of the United States. The first Americans to visit Alta California were seamen, followed later by the pathfinders and mountain men who opened up the West.

Antap: A Chumash religious cult, keepers of sacred knowledge.

Apostolic College: See Missionary College

Apse: a domed or vaulted semicircular recess, found most frequently at the east end of a church.

Arroyo: A brook rivulet or small stream.

Asistencia: A sub-mission having residents, converted Indians, but no resident missionary.

Asphaltum: Naturally occurring gluey tar used by the Chumash for waterproofing canoes and baskets.

Atole: A maize (cornmeal) gruel or porridge.

Baja: Lower, as in Baja California, the peninsula that is part of Mexico, directly south of Alta California.

Balustrade: A low barrier (made of carved and painted wooden spindles and a railing) often created in the mission churches.

Baroque: 17th century style of artistic expression characterized by elaborate ornamentation and dynamic forms.

Barranca: A deep ravine or canyon.

Basilica: A Roman Catholic Church of special historical and religious importance.

Bear Flag Revolt: The armed uprising by a band of Americans that started on June 14, 1846, leading to the declaration of the independent California Republic. Within a month, the United States occupied Monterey and California officially became part of the United States in 1848 with the Treaty of Guadalupe Hidalgo.

Bee-hive oven: A wood-fired cone-shaped over used for baking bread.

Bodega: A cellar, wine cellar or wine vault.

Bota: A leather container consisting of a single cowhide used for storing or shipping tallow. The contents weighed about 200 pounds.

Bulto: A carved, painted three-dimensional figure usually set in a recess. Most of the mission churches featured a bulto depicting the saint for whom the mission is named.

Buttresses: Supporting structures built into a standing wall to strengthen it.

Caballero: Man on horseback.

Cabo: Corporal

Californios: Native-born Californians of full or partial Hispanic heritage.

Campanario: Bell tower. Can be free standing or attached.

Campo Santo: Literally means "Holy Field." The cemetery.

Canaliño: A name used by European explorers and settlers to identify Chumash peoples who lived in the Santa Barbara Channel area. The word is also used today by some researchers to refer to the group of Native Americans who lived in the Channel area thousands of years ago and who are probably ancestors of the Chumash.

Candeleros: Candlesticks in Spanish.

Cañón: Canyon

Cantor: A singer in church services, which was often a neophyte Indian.

Calinche: A drink made from the fruit of the prickly pear or tuna cactus.

Capilla: A chapel.

Carreta: Wooden, two-wheeled cart, pulled by oxen. The cart was the principal mode of transporting items in Alta California.

Casa-reales: Government buildings, town hall.

Castas: People of mixed blood, as opposed to Spanish and Indians.

Cemetery: The formal burial grounds for the remains of the dead. Most of the mission cemeteries were sited adjacent to the mission church.

Cenotaph: A monument erected to honor someone whose mortal remains are elsewhere.

Chancel: The area in a church containing the altar and seats for the clergy.

Channel Indians: The natives living in the Santa Barbara area.

Cocinero: A cook, probably for the priest, since this was normally not a normal male occupation within the Indian population.

Colaterales: The side altars in a church.

Commandante: Military commander.

Commissary Prefect: An office established in California in 1812 to assist the Father President in the supervision of missionaries and liaison with the territorial government.

Comissionado: A deputy or commissioner. As normally used in California, he was a non-commissioned officer serving on detached duty as a magistrate of a pueblo or villa.

Compound: A cluster of connected buildings. Most missions were built as a quadrangle that included a church, padre's quarters and workshops, with native quarters, warehouses and other buildings surrounding the central compound.

Convento: The padre's residence in the mission complex.

Corridor: A long walkway or gallery around the inner patio. These were usually arched or colonnaded.

Crioles: Spaniards born in the New World.

Cuera: Protective several-ply leather jacket, usually sleeveless and of thigh-length.

Cupola: A small rounded structure built on top of a roof or bell tower.

Dado: Decorative border appearing on the lower portion of the interior wall of a church.

Diputacion: Elected assembly, which met at Monterey during the Mexican rule of Alta California.

Don: Form of respectful address once used only for the nobility, but relaxed subsequently. The proper use is with the given or full name, never with surname alone.

El Camino Real: Technically, the "Royal Highway" a term used to designate the main road in a Spanish territory. In Alta California, El Camino Real was a dirt road that linked the missions and extended from San Diego to Sonoma. U.S. 101 roughly parallels El Camino Real.

Enfermero: An Indian male nurse who tended the numerous sick at the mission.

Enramada: Temporary brush shelter.

Entrada: Entrance.

Escolta: The military guard assigned from a nearby presidio for mission or pueblo protection. It consisted of a corporal and from 5 to 7 soldiers.

Escopeta: A short carbine carried by most Spanish soldiers.

Espadana: Separate pierced bell-wall such as that found at Mission San Diego or Mission San Gabriel.

Estadal: Spanish linear measurement of about 3.3 meters, or 11 feet.

Fandango: Lively regional Spanish dance and its music.

Fanega: Dry measure of weight the equivalent of about 1.6 bushels.

Fiesta: A gathering of people to celebrate an event, such as a Saint's Day, the anniversary of the mission etc. The Chumash also held fiestas before the arrival of the Europeans. During Chumash fiestas people traded goods and played games, and the village leaders conducted business.

245

Founders: Padres and principal Spanish authorities that first settled Alta California and established the missions.

Franciscan: Member of the Catholic religious order founded by Saint Francis of Assisi in 1209. Franciscans are dedicated to preaching, missionary work and charitable acts.

Fray: Member of a mendicant (begging) order, such as the Franciscans. Could be a priest or lay brother. Should only be used with the man's full name, not with the surname. (Jesuits were not frays.)

Fresco: A painting laid down on moist lime plaster with color pigments suspended in a liquid medium.

Frigate: In mission days a frigate was a three-masted sailing ship. In most navies, a frigate is the smallest surface combatant that can conduct extended blue-water missions. The raid on Alta California in 1818 was led by frigate, La Argentina, a 677-ton vessel outfitted with 34 eight- and 12-caliber guns, and carrying a crew of about 260 men.

Gente de Razon: Literally, educated people. A phrase used to characterize those who followed Spanish customs. Used to designate non-Indians.

Fandango: Lively regional Spanish dance and its music.

Fanega: A fanega is approximately 1.575 bushels. For Spanish measurement it is also 12 almundes.

Fiesta: A gathering of people to celebrate an event, such as a Saint's Day, the anniversary of the mission etc. The Chumash also held fiestas before the arrival of the Europeans. During Chumash fiestas people traded goods and played games, and the village leaders conducted business.

Founders: Padres and principal Spanish authorities that first settled Alta California and established the missions.

Franciscan: Member of the Catholic religious order founded by Saint Francis of Assisi in 1209. Franciscans are dedicated to preaching, missionary work and charitable acts.

Fray: Member of a mendicant (begging) order, such as the Franciscans. Could be a priest or lay brother. Should only be used with the man's full name, not with the surname. (Jesuits were not frays.)

Fresco: A painting laid down on moist lime plaster with color pigments suspended in a liquid medium.

Frigate: In mission days a frigate was a three-masted sailing ship. In most navies, a frigate is the smallest surface combatant that can conduct extended blue-water missions. The raid on Alta California in 1818 was led by frigate, La Argentina, a 677-ton vessel outfitted with 34 eight- and 12-caliber guns, and carrying a crew of about 260 men.

Gente de Razon: Literally, educated people. A phrase used to characterize those who followed Spanish customs. Used to designate non-Indians.

Governor: The senior official appointed to administer an area. California was initially governed from Loreto, Mexico, but the seat of government moved to Monterey in 1777. During the Mexican period the seat of government shifted several times as northern and southern factions vied for control.

Habit: Garb worn by members of a religious community or order. In Alta California the Franciscans wore a gray habit.

Hidalgo: Member of Spain's lowest-ranking nobility.

Iglesia: Church.

Informe: A general term which refers to the annual report of the state of a mission district.

Jacal: A hut or crude dwelling often made of brush and hides.

Ladrillo: A tile floor.

Lagar: A wine, olive, or apple press.

Lavanderia: Laundry.

Legua: Standard Spanish measure of distance for a league, equal to 2.597 miles. There were 5,000 varas in a legua.

Letter of Marque: The papers given a privateer authorizing him to act. The letter specified the period for which it was valid. Often the limits of the Marque were vague, leaving it up to the captain and crew to determine where to go and what they could seize.

Madrina: Godmother

Majordomo: A mayordomo served as a custodian of civic property, also a foreman of a hacienda or mission. An overseer.

Mendicant Order: Religious organizations which have renounced all common and personal property. Thus, members are dependent upon begging in order to survive.

Merced de Tierra: Land grant.

Mestizo: Mixed-blood of European and Indian ancestry.

Metate: A flat slab of rock used to grind seeds, nuts and plant foods into flour.

Mexican-American War: Armed conflict between the United States and Mexico that lasted from 1846 to 1848. Led to annexation of 58 percent of Mexican territory including Texas, New Mexico, Arizona and California.

Michumash: The word from which the term Chumash originated. It refers to those people who lived on Santa Cruz Island.

Milpa: A plot of land, grain field, or corn field.

Mission Vieja: Literally means Old Mission. This is the term used for the first site of Mission La Purísima Concepcíon which was destroyed by the earthquake of 1812.

Missionary College: Franciscan institutions established to receive and train priests for service in the missions. The missions of Alta California were sponsored by the College of San Fernando founded in 1734 in Mexico City.

Molino: A grist-mill.

Monjerio: Woman's quarters.

Native Americans: The indigenous people living in a land. The Indian natives of Alta California lived in the area for several thousand years before the arrival of the Europeans.

Nave: The principal interior of a church, where the congregation worships.

Neophytes: Indians who were converted to Christianity and then lived at a mission.

New Spain: Present day Mexico, with its headquarters in Mexico City.

Nicho: A recess designed to hold a statue. Can be free standing, or part of a reredo.

Novitiate: Religious house where beginners (novices) are trained before taking permanent vows.

Padre: A Roman Catholic priest.

Padrino: Godfather.

Padrón: A mission register of neophyte families which was like a census.

Page or *Paje:* An Indian house-servant for the mission fathers.

Panadero: A baker or bread-maker.

Paqwot: Chumash term referring to the leader of several villages.

Pathfinder: An early explorer who established trails in un-charted territory.

Plaza: A rectangular central public area. All of the Spanish pueblos (towns) and most of the missions included a plaza.

Poblador: Original Hispanic settler.

Polychrome: Decorated with several colors.

Portal: A gate or doorway.

Pozole: A porridge or thick soup of wheat, corn, beans or horse beans and meat.

President (of the Missions): Chief Religious Official in the mission territory, appointed by the apostolic college of which he was a member. After 1812, some of the responsibilities were taken over by a Commisary Prefect.

Presidio: Fortified military outpost or fort. The Spanish presidios in Alta California included barracks, workshops, stables and a chapel.

Privateer: A privately owned vessel armed and equipped at the owner's expense, for the purpose of carrying on a maritime war by the authority of one of the belligerent parties. The privateer was authorized to appropriate captured property. The men who sailed on one of the vessels were also called privateers.

Procurator: Friar appointed to take care of business matters. The procurator of San Fernando College purchased supplies for the California missions.

Pueblo: The non-Indian towns established to help colonize Alta California.

Pulpit (pulpito in Spanish): Raised platform in a church used for preaching. The sounding board or canopy over the pulpit is called the tornavoz in Spanish.

Quadrangle: Four-sided enclosure. Most missions were laid out using a quadrangle design.

Rancheria: Spanish word for an Indian village.

Rancho: Separate establishment, typically devoted to agriculture and/or the management of livestock.

Rectory: Clergy's residence.

Refectory: The dining area in a mission.

Reliquary: Sealed metal and glass receptacle for displaying sacred objects.

Remate: The front wall of a mission church, similar to an espadana, but without openings for bells. It may contain a niche for a statue.

Reredos: Structure placed behind the altar table and against the wall, typically sub-divided into panels and nichos, and richly decorated.

Restoration: The process of rebuilding a structure, using to the extent possible, original plans, material and tools.

Runaways: Neophytes who escaped from a mission. A concerted effort was made to recapture all runaways, often with military excursions into the interior during the 1820s-1830s, when missions were under pressure to maintain production as the neophyte population declined.

Sacristan: An individual having charge of the sacristy of the church.

Sacristy: Room off the sanctuary containing priest garments and other articles used in church services.

Sala: Formal reception room; an area in the mission used to receive guests and visitors.

Sanctuary: Part of the church containing the altar.

Scurvy: A condition resulting from a lack of ascorbic acid (Vitamin C). Common among sailors due to an inadequate intake of fresh fruits and vegetables. Many of the sailors on the Portola expedition of 1769 died of scurvy.

Secularization: The process under which the Mexican government removed the mission lands from the jurisdiction of the Franciscans (who were replaced by secular priests) and half the mission land theoretically turned over to the Indians. The bylaws for secularization were enacted by the Mexican Congress in 1828, ratified in 1833 and fully enforced in 1834.

Shaman: Medicine man responsible in an Indian tribe for curing disease and contacting the spiritual world.

Soldados de Cuera: The term used to describe the Spanish soldiers on the frontier; named after their distinctive reinforced leather jacket. According to regulations, the jackets were to be made out of seven layers of buckskin, and were designed to stop an Indian arrow.

Tabernacle (sangrario in Spanish): Ornamental receptacle placed in the center of the altar and used to hold consecrated wafers.

Tasajo: Spanish term for jerked beef which was used extensively at the missions.

Temescal: Spanish word for an Indian sweathouse, used exclusively by men for both religious and non-religious purposes.

Temporarilities: Matters pertaining to the non-religious aspects of the mission: Feeding, clothing and housing of the Indians; development of agriculture; teaching of trades and skills.

Third Order of St. Francis: Organization of lay people who emulate and follow the teachings of St. Francis, but who do not give up marriage or worldly possessions.

Tile: The tiles used at the mission were made on the premises from clay shaped over log molds, and then fired in a kiln.

Tok: Milkweed fiber used to make strings for a bow.

Tomol: Plank canoe made by the Chumash Indians.

Transept: That part of a cruciform church that crosses at right angles between the nave and the apse.

Treaty of Guadelupe Hidalgo: The 1848 agreement between Mexico and the United States that ended the Mexican War, and ceded 58 percent of Mexican territory, including Alta California, to the United States.

Tribe: A society consisting of several communities united by kinship, culture, language and other social institutions.

Vaquero: Cowboy, cattle hand.

Vara: Spanish unit of measure, considered the Spanish yard. In Mexico and California a vara equaled 32.9 inches. It was equivalent to 2.7424 feet in colonial California.

Vigas: Ceiling beams, used as the primary support for the roof of a building.

Viña: Another term for vineyard.

Vicar Forane: Ecclesiastical official appointed by a bishop and having limited jurisdiction over a portion of a diocese.

Vicar General: Priest deputized to assist the bishop with ordinary jurisdiction of an entire diocese.

Viceroy: Officials who were appointed by the King of Spain for one year at a time, and who were held responsible for civil, religious and military affairs within vast overseas dominions. The missions in Alta California were under the authority of the Viceroy of New Spain (Mexico) located in Mexico City.

Vigas: Ceiling beams, used as the primary support for the roof of a building.

Viña: Another term for vineyard.

Visitador-General: Friar appointed by the General of an Order to conduct a formal inspection of a province or apostolic college.

Wot: Chumash word for chief.

Yankee Dollars: Cured cattle hides used by the missions to trade with ships.

Ynterprete: An interpreter who aided the priest in preaching to the Indians.

Zanja: Spanish name for ditch used for irrigation.

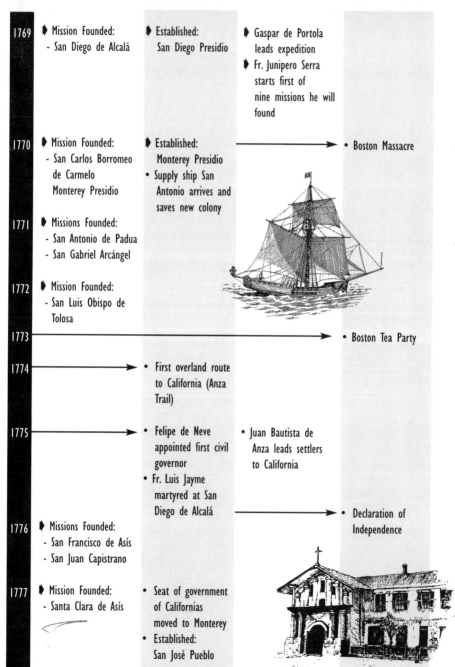

CALIFORNIA MISSIONS
―――― TIME LINE ――――

1769
- ▶ Mission Founded:
  - San Diego de Alcalá
- ▶ Established:
  San Diego Presidio
- ▶ Gaspar de Portola leads expedition
- ▶ Fr. Junipero Serra starts first of nine missions he will found

1770
- ▶ Mission Founded:
  - San Carlos Borromeo de Carmelo
  Monterey Presidio
- ▶ Established:
  Monterey Presidio
- • Supply ship San Antonio arrives and saves new colony
- • Boston Massacre

1771
- ▶ Missions Founded:
  - San Antonio de Padua
  - San Gabriel Arcángel

1772
- ▶ Mission Founded:
  - San Luis Obispo de Tolosa

1773
- • Boston Tea Party

1774
- • First overland route to California (Anza Trail)

1775
- • Felipe de Neve appointed first civil governor
- • Fr. Luis Jayme martyred at San Diego de Alcalá
- • Juan Bautista de Anza leads settlers to California
- • Declaration of Independence

1776
- ▶ Missions Founded:
  - San Francisco de Asís
  - San Juan Capistrano

1777
- ▶ Mission Founded:
  - Santa Clara de Asís
- • Seat of government of Californias moved to Monterey
- • Established:
  San José Pueblo

253

CALIFORNIA MISSIONS
TIME LINE

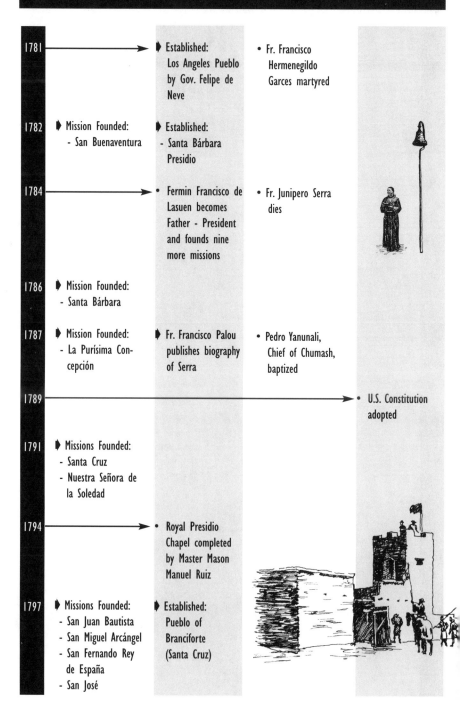

1781 — Established:
Los Angeles Pueblo
by Gov. Felipe de
Neve

• Fr. Francisco
Hermenegildo
Garces martyred

1782 ▶ Mission Founded:
- San Buenaventura

▶ Established:
- Santa Bárbara
Presidio

1784 — • Fermin Francisco de
Lasuen becomes
Father - President
and founds nine
more missions

• Fr. Junipero Serra
dies

1786 ▶ Mission Founded:
- Santa Bárbara

1787 ▶ Mission Founded:
- La Purísima Con-
cepción

▶ Fr. Francisco Palou
publishes biography
of Serra

• Pedro Yanunali,
Chief of Chumash,
baptized

1789 — • U.S. Constitution
adopted

1791 ▶ Missions Founded:
- Santa Cruz
- Nuestra Señora de
la Soledad

1794 — • Royal Presidio
Chapel completed
by Master Mason
Manuel Ruiz

1797 ▶ Missions Founded:
- San Juan Bautista
- San Miguel Arcángel
- San Fernando Rey
de España
- San José

▶ Established:
Pueblo of
Branciforte
(Santa Cruz)

254

CALIFORNIA MISSIONS
TIME LINE

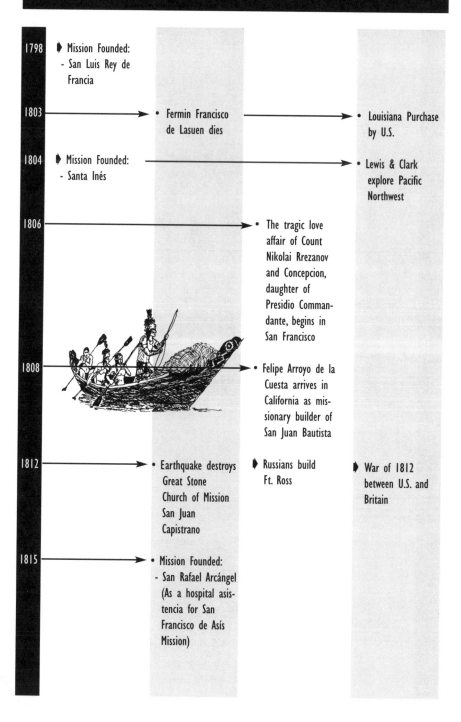

1798 ▶ Mission Founded:
- San Luis Rey de Francia

1803 • Fermin Francisco de Lasuen dies

• Louisiana Purchase by U.S.

1804 ▶ Mission Founded:
- Santa Inés

• Lewis & Clark explore Pacific Northwest

1806 • The tragic love affair of Count Nikolai Rrezanov and Concepcion, daughter of Presidio Commandante, begins in San Francisco

1808 • Felipe Arroyo de la Cuesta arrives in California as missionary builder of San Juan Bautista

1812 • Earthquake destroys Great Stone Church of Mission San Juan Capistrano

▶ Russians build Ft. Ross

▶ War of 1812 between U.S. and Britain

1815 • Mission Founded:
- San Rafael Arcángel (As a hospital asistencia for San Francisco de Asís Mission)

CALIFORNIA MISSIONS
─── TIME LINE ───

1817 ▸ Mission Founded:
- San Rafael Arcángel
(As a hospital
asistencia for
San Francisco de Asís
Mission)

1818 • Founded:
- San Isabel
Asistencia
(Sub-mission of
Mission San Diego)

▸ Pirate Hipolite
Bouchard attacks
California, burns
Monterey
Presidio & Mission
San Juan
Capistrano

1821 ▸ Mexico wins inde-
pendence from Spain
and takes control
of missions

1823 ▸ Mission Founded:
- San Francisco Solano
• San Rafael given full
mission status

1826 • Jedediah Strong
Smith, legendary
Mountain Man, is
first American to
reach California
by land

1827 • Captain Duhaut-Cilly
visits California on
world trip and
publishes impres-
sions in 1833-1834

1829 • Indian Neophyte
Estanislao ends
long revolt and
returns to
San José Mission

1834 • Missions secularized
(1833-1834)

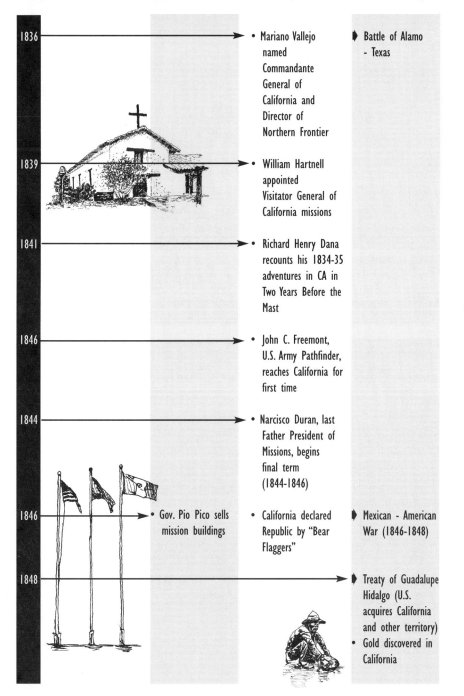

CALIFORNIA MISSIONS
TIME LINE

1836 • Mariano Vallejo named Commandante General of California and Director of Northern Frontier

▶ Battle of Alamo - Texas

1839 • William Hartnell appointed Visitator General of California missions

1841 • Richard Henry Dana recounts his 1834-35 adventures in CA in Two Years Before the Mast

257

1846 • John C. Freemont, U.S. Army Pathfinder, reaches California for first time

1844 • Narcisco Duran, last Father President of Missions, begins final term (1844-1846)

1846 • Gov. Pio Pico sells mission buildings

• California declared Republic by "Bear Flaggers"

▶ Mexican - American War (1846-1848)

1848
▶ Treaty of Guadalupe Hidalgo (U.S. acquires California and other territory)

• Gold discovered in California

REFERENCES

The Spell of California's Spanish Colonial Missions, by Donald Francis Toomey. Particularly useful for the definition of architectural and religious terms.

Spain in the Southwest by John L. Kessell. Glossary contains concise definition of Spanish terms used during the period.

Illustrated Glossary of Terms Relating to California Missions and Other Hispanic Sites http://www.ca-missions.org/illusgl.html. An Internet site developed by Sasha Honig. Contains illustrations, examples and extensive explanations.

The Chumash by Robert O. Gibson. Concise definitions of Native-American terms.

Franciscan Missionaries in Hispanic California by Maynard Geiger. The glossary contains definitions of terms used by the Catholic Church, the Franciscan order and Spanish authorities during the mission period.

On-line Dictionary of Spanish, http://www.spanishdict.com/

Lands of Promise and Despair, edited by Rose Marie Beebe and Robert M. Senkewicz. An excellent reference source.

INDEX

A

Aguirre, Don Antonio xv, 85, 148-152, 237
Alvarado, Juan Bautista 104, 115
Anza, Juan Bautista de xiii, 2-3, 30-36, 235
Arguello, Maria de la Conception Marcela 70-73
Arroyo xii, xiv, 84, 89, 90, 91, 93, 236

B

Bancroft, Hubert Howe vii, 29, 45, 99, 106, 108, 152
Bear Flag Revolt 105, 162, 166, 242
Bouchard, Hipolite xii, xiv, 5, 74-82, 103, 236

C

Cabrillo, Juan Rodriguez xiii, 1-2, 6-12, 15, 235
California Landmarks Club xv, 175, 177-178, 201, 216, 220
California Mission Studies Association viii, ix
Carmel, Mission (see also Carmelo, San Carlos Borremeo de) viii, x, xiii, xvi, 2, 4, 24, 28, 33, 60-66, 92, 114, 163, 196, 197, 207, 222-233, 238, 239
Carmelo, San Carlos Borremeo de 2, 24, 63, 223, 229, 233
Chapman, Joseph 127
Chumash Indians xiii, 3, 8, 42, 43, 45-52, 235, 241, 244, 248, 249, 250

Connell, Will 197, 199
Corney, Peter 77, 80, 81
Cortez, Hernan 9
Crespi, Juan (Fr.) 17, 18, 224
Crump, Spencer vii, 204, 238
Cuesta, Felipe Arroyo de la (Fr.) xii, xiv, 84, 89-93, 236

D

Dana, Richard Henry xi, xv, 85, 132-139, 144, 237
Davies, Marion 217-219, 238
Deakin, Edwin viii, xvi, 163, 188, 189, 191-193, 238
Diego y Moreno, Francisco Garcia (Bishop) 149, 151
Doak, Thomas 91
Dolores, Mission (See also San Francisco de Asis) 68, 92, 95, 102, 144, 231
Downie, Harry xvi, 163, 223, 228-233, 238, 239
Drake, Sir Francis 1
Duhaut-Cilly, Auguste xiv, 85, 118-123, 236
Duran, Narcisso (Fr.) xv, 85, 95-96, 141-147, 149, 151, 237

E

El Camino Real xvi, 31, 42, 163, 195, 200-205, 238, 243
Engelhardt, Zephyrin (Fr.) vii, 91, 93, 99
Estanislao xii, xiv, 84, 94-99, 101, 236

F

Fiske, George x, 183
Forbes, Mrs. A.S.C. vii, xvi, 163, 200-205, 238

Ford, Henry Chapman xvi, 163, 189-190, 193, 238
Fort Ross 71-72, 74
Franciscan Order vii, xi, xiii, xiv, 3, 4, 17, 22, 23, 25, 29, 32, 45, 54, 55, 57, 58, 84, 85, 89, 90, 91, 92, 93, 126, 127, 141, 145, 146, 147, 187, 189, 202, 207, 224, 231, 238, 244, 245, 250
Fremont, John Charles xi, xv, 162, 166-173, 237

G
Galvez, Jose de 15
Garces, Francisco Hermenegildo (Fr.) xi, xiii, 4, 32, 55-59, 126, 235
Geiger, Maynard (Fr.) vii, 25, 29, 45, 58, 92, 93, 146, 147, 250
Gold Rush 72, 107

H
Hardwick, Michael vii, 43, 48, 52, 235
Harte, Bret 72, 73, 226
Hartnell, William xiv, 84, 104, 110-117, 236
Hathaway, Pat viii, 237, 238, 239
Hearst, William Randolph xi, xvi, 163, 164, 214-220, 238
Hide Trade xi, 5, 7, 2, 85, 132, 133, 134, 136, 137-138, 143, 150, 249
Hunter-Liggett Military Reservation 218, 219

I
Independence of California 105
Independence of Mexico 104, 150, 155

Indians xii, 2, 7, 8, 9, 17, 24, 26, 33, 39, 42, 43, 44, 45, 46, 48, 50, 51, 52, 55, 56, 57, 58, 59, 61, 62, 63, 77, 83, 84, 85, 89, 90, 93, 96, 97, 98, 99, 101, 102, 103, 111, 113, 114, 120, 122, 126, 129, 130, 137, 141, 142, 143, 144, 146, 155, 156, 162, 183, 184, 185, 205, 209, 225, 241, 242, 243, 244, 246, 248

J
Jackson, Helen Hunt (author of *Ramona*) xv, 162, 182-187, 201, 237
Jayme, Luis (Fr.) 55, 123
Jesuits 16, 27, 244
Jorgensen, Christian August xvi, 163, 189-191

L
La Purisima 43, 49, 51, 94, 178
Lasuen, Fermin Francisco 25
Los Angeles, El Pueblo de la Reina de 3, 42, 133
Lummis, Charles Fletcher xv, 162, 163, 174-181, 201, 220, 237

M
McGroarty, John Steven xvi, 163, 180, 206-212, 238
Miller, Henry 172, 236
Moncada, Fernando Rivera y 17
Monterey, Royal Presidio Chapel xiii, 61-65, 67, 77, 103, 236
Monterey, Presidio xiv, 2, 4, 5, 6, 14, 16, 19, 32, 34, 47, 61, 62, 75, 76, 78, 81, 103, 104

Mora, Josephy Jacinto "Jo" xvi, 163, 222-227, 238

Munras, Estevan xiii, 4, 61-66, 236

N

Native Daughters of the Golden West 230

Neve, Phillipe de xiii, 3, 38-45, 48, 235

O

Otis, Harrison Gray 175, 176, 177, 208

P

Pico, Pio xii, xv, 85, 111, 112, 115, 145, 154-160, 167, 170, 237

Portola, Don Gaspar de xiii, 2, 15-20, 23, 24, 27, 47, 215, 226, 235, 248

R

Rezanov, Count Nikolai Petrovich xiv, 4, 68-73, 236

Ruiz, Manuel xiii, 4, 60-66, 78, 236

S

San Antonia de Pala (Asistencia) 178

San Antonio de Padua (Mission) xi, 2, 33, 164, 174, 214-220, 230

San Buenaventura (Mission) 3, 11, 42, 48, 163, 230

San Carlos Borromeo de Carmelo (Mission Carmel) viii, x, xiii, xvi, 2, 4, 24, 28, 33, 60-66, 92, 114, 163, 196, 197, 207, 222-233, 238, 239

San Diego de Alcala (Mission) 2, 4, 18-19, 23, 31, 39, 47, 55, 134, 149, 150, 152, 244

San Fernando Rey (Mission) ii, 157, 170, 178

San Francisco Solano (Mission) 27, 100, 104, 112

San Gabriel (Mission) 2, 30, 31, 33, 34, 42, 56, 99, 126, 127, 128, 129, 149, 156, 160, 163, 206, 207, 236, 244

San Jose (Mission) xii, xiv, 95, 96, 98, 114, 141-144, 195, 225, 231, 237

San Jose (Pueblo) 3, 41, 97

San Juan Bautista (Mission) 89, 91-93, 144, 163, 220, 230, 236

San Juan Capistrano xii, xiv, 5, 39, 54, 75, 77, 78, 127, 134, 148-149, 157, 178, 207

San Luis Obispo 12, 33, 39, 110, 113, 117, 145, 157, 163, 194, 230

San Luis Rey 111, 124, 150, 157, 158, 172, 178, 187, 198, 238

San Miguel (Mission) xii, xiii, 4, 59, 61, 63, 64, 144, 159, 200, 237

San Rafael Acangel (Mission) 144, 188

Santa Barbara (Mission) 11, 43, 49, 52, 85, 123, 134, 140, 144, 151, 235

Santa Barbara (Pueblo) 3, 38, 42, 48, 51, 119, 133

Santa Clara (Mission) 92, 196

Santa Cruz (Mission) 11, 76, 144, 191, 238

Santa Inez 4, 49, 51, 92, 118, 157, 182

Secularization xv, 85, 92, 102, 111, 141, 145, 146, 147, 152, 155, 156, 158, 160, 248

Serra, Junipero (Fr.) xi, xiii, xvi, 2-3, 16-19, 22-29, 42-44, 48, 56, 61, 62, 102, 106, 157, 163, 187, 196, 205, 207, 209, 215, 223-226, 230, 231, 232, 233, 235, 238, 240

Settlement 3, 4, 19, 24, 40, 48, 95, 103, 104, 215

Smith, Jedidiah Strong xv, 85, 124-131, 190, 203, 236

Sola, Pablo Vicente de 75-76, 78, 112, 155

Soledad (Mission) 104, 123, 147, 163, 230

T

Tapis, Estevan (Fr.) 89

Toomey, Donald Francis viii, 64, 66, 157, 160, 250

U

U.S. Army xv, 169-171, 184, 224, 225

V

Vallejo, Guadelupe 93

Vallejo, Mariano xiv, 72, 84, 96, 99, 100-108, 112, 155, 168, 169, 236

Vroman, Adam Clark 163, 196, 199, 238

W

Watkins, Carleton E. 163, 195, 197-198, 199, 238

William Randolph Hearst Foundation 230

Y

Yanunali, Pedro xiii, 3, 46-52, 235

Yuman Indians 57

Pentacle Press
P.O. Box 9400
Scottsdale, AZ 85252

PLEASE SEND ME THE FOLLOWING:

QUAN.	ITEM	PRICE
_____	*Soldiers, Scoundrels, Poets & Priests* Paperback $17.95 ea.	_____
	AZ residents add 7.7% Sales Tax) SALES TAX	_____
	($3.50 for first book, then $.50 for each add'l book)	
	SHIPPING	_____
	TOTAL	_____

NAME

COMPANY NAME

ADDRESS

MAILING ADDRESS *(IF DIFFERENT FROM ABOVE)*

CITY   STATE   ZIP

HOME TELEPHONE   FAX   EMAIL

PAYMENT:

❑ Checks payable to *Pentacle Press* and mail to:
    P. O. Box 9400, Scottsdale, AZ 85252

❑ VISA ❑ MasterCard ❑ AMEX ❑ Discover

Cardnumber:_____

Name on card:_____

Exp. Date: _____ (mo) _____(year)

■ Secure Fax orders: 480-443-9333. Fill out this form & fax.

■ On-line orders: www.pentaclestore.com
    orders@www.missionscalifornia.com